D0951891

Poems That Touch The Heart

POEMS

That Touch The Heart

NEW, ENLARGED EDITION

COMPILED BY

A. L. ALEXANDER

Creator and Conductor of:
The Good Will Court
The *original* Mediation Board
The Court of Human Relations

DOUBLEDAY
NEW YORK LONDON TORONTO SYDNEY AUCKLAND

PUBLISHED BY DOUBLEDAY
a division of Bantam Doubleday Dell Publishing Group, Inc.
1540 Broadway, New York, New York 10036

DOUBLEDAY and the portrayal of an anchor with a dolphin
are registered trademarks of Doubleday,
a division of Bantam Doubleday Dell Publishing Group, Inc.

ISBN 0-385-04401-1
Library of Congress Catalog Number 56-11498
Copyright © 1941, 1956 by Doubleday,
a division of Bantam Doubleday Dell Publishing Group, Inc.
PRINTED IN THE UNITED STATES OF AMERICA

40   41

CONTENTS

Contents

Contents

Contents

Contents

Contents

Contents

Contents

Contents

Contents

Contents

Contents

Contents

Contents

PREFACE TO NEW,
ENLARGED EDITION

In the noisy confusion of today's high-pressure world, against the great canvas of economics and politics and far-reaching world affairs, there is a tendency to overlook the "abstraction" known as the human being.

The turbulence in today's living, the tense struggle for survival, tends to make life hard and men cruel. Notwithstanding the breaking of the sound barrier, the splitting of the atom, and such projects as million-pound rockets to the moon or man-made satellites encircling the earth, the most challenging—surely the most distressing—problem of our time is "Man's inhumanity to Man."

Warmth, tenderness, understanding, kindness, love, affection—these are terms which so often seem strangely out of tune in the jangled age in which we live. Even the common courtesies appear close to being "lost in the shuffle." To be realistic, respect for the dignity in human personality has been diminishing to an alarming degree.

The fashionable thing is to be cynical, to jibe at sentiment, to hide from others one's being affected by pity or sympathy or love. The risk is to draw derisive attention if one is thought naive or sentimental. "The law of grab," the most hard-bitten and callous materialism seem to be the prevailing order, often devoid of the slightest semblance of principle or decency or honor.

How saddening that machinery has been developed that

gives us abundance, but has left us in want; that knowledge has made us cynical; that cleverness has made us hard and unkind. What is needed more than machinery is humanity; kindness and gentleness far more than cleverness.

The great experience of life is of course the quest of every heart for a measure of happiness and security; the great secret is to find some philosophy to sustain us in time of trouble and disappointment. This is the end of religion, the object of philosophy, the pursuit of the whole world.

Symptomatic of our time is the tendency to lose any real sense of the meaning and purpose of life, to hold cheap or distort the most precious values that life affords. Anyone dealing with any phase of human relations today will testify to the staggering number of people living uncertain, disorganized lives with fears and worries so intensified that ours is labeled "The Age of Tension and Anxiety."

Where there is no faith in life's essential worthwhileness, nothing to turn to, nothing to hang on to, no philosophy to give a reasonable answer, it is small wonder that disillusionment, frustration, discouragement, add up to the nation's startling toll of emotional and mental illness.

Our natures are so open to suggestion from our surroundings. When we read or hear so much of the news of crimes and corruption it is not strange that there develops a besetting consciousness of cynicism and disaster. When we expose ourselves to concepts that are elevating and invigorating, our horizons begin to lift, our hardness of heart begins to soften, our gloom begins to lighten.

Thus it was that during the early days of broadcasting I began the custom of concluding each of my programs with a human interest poem that seemed to have the capacity for strengthening faith or rekindling hope. How many times had I been lured from a maze of doubt, infused with new spirit, because of some comforting or inspiring word from the Poets. It seemed to me that poetry of such pertinent nature was not only appealing because of its aptness, pleasurable because of its form, but that it said more in fewer words than prose and was indeed the simplest and most effective way of expressing a thought.

The extraordinary audience response, indicated by the sacks of mail requesting copies of poems that struck a responsive chord, resulted in the original compilation of POEMS THAT TOUCH THE HEART. Since its publication (there have been some thirty-one reprintings numbering over 400,-000 copies) my publishers have continually urged me to compile a revised and enlarged edition of POEMS THAT TOUCH THE HEART comprising the additional human interest material collected and utilized on the air during the ensuing years. Most of this material has never before been available in published form.

In offering this new, revised and enlarged edition it is my conviction that today especially the urgent need of people is to find something to believe in, something that sustains in time of trial or crisis, something that takes a person out of himself, identifies him with a life larger and beyond himself.

This, then, is poetry that looks into the heart of things, strengthens our interest in human nature, elevates the drooping spirit, intensifies our aspiration toward the good and the beautiful in all that surrounds us, and tends to raise the level of our lives by helping us to see the essentials of life more clearly.

Preface to New Enlarged Edition

May you, in turning these pages, experience as I have, that sudden pleasurable quiver of recognition that announces the particular message sought after, discover something that truly warms and touches the heart.

It is my earnest hope that this volume may contribute in some measure to the cultivation of that larger vision which helps us to "see life steadily and see it whole."

A. L. ALEXANDER

INTRODUCTION

And if a lowly singer dries one tear,
Or soothes one humble human heart in pain,
Be sure his homely verse to God is dear,
And not one stanza has been sung in vain.

Some years ago, when one of our great public buildings was nearing completion, the president of a leading university was invited to prepare a set of quotations to be inscribed upon the walls of the foyer in expression of the highest meaning of law, religion, art, philosophy, science, literature, industry and other central activities of the life of man. He experienced no great difficulty until he came to the field of ethics and some expression dealing with the ideal ends of human action and a noble standard for one's life. Lofty precepts from the Old and New Testaments were for his purposes restricted to the panel on religion.

While he found many expressions accepted the world over as exalted statements of morality, he passed them all by, finally to place high upon the walls the simple declaration "civilization is just the slow process of learning to be kind." Below was inscribed a familiar verse by a popular American poet.

So many gods, so many creeds,
So many paths that wind and wind,
When just the art of being kind
Is all this sad world needs.

Introduction

Surely among the benefactors of mankind are those who condense life's significant and essential principles into a form easily impressed upon the memory.

Plato said that "poetry is nearer to vital truth than history." It is not unreasonable to conclude that if a maddened world suddenly were to find destroyed all encyclopedias and textbooks, it would somehow survive if there were preserved the poetry that "plucks the string with just the touch the human heart craves," and while we may not care for literature as such, there is a kind of writing, the personal outcries wrung from men and women in the strong twist of life, to which we cannot remain indifferent. Surely the most quotable things that have come down to us through the ages have been poems, and yet there are those editors, by and large, who use poetry, if at all, merely as "a filler," on the ground that the public does not want it. It has been my privilege to be one of those able to disprove this popular misconception as to the extent of the public interest in poetry, the art which was called by Coleridge "the blossom and the fragrance of all human knowledge, human thoughts, human passions, emotions, language."

My experience in the broadcasting field has been devoted for the most part to the presentation of human-interest programs dealing with the joys and sorrows, the hopes and responsibilities which form the chief interest of human life. Throughout this experience I have been impressed by the surprisingly large numbers of people who feel the absence of human contacts, the sympathy of common experience and common understanding which people crave as naturally as sun and air. I have found that programs dealing with the essential truths of life, those which have a tendency to inspire patience of heart and strength of mind, can make an amazingly real contribution to the lives of many. These real-life programs, aside from any other consideration, have given me an insight into some of the hopes and aspirations of people in their search for happiness, clouded by shadows of misunderstanding and strife.

Especially in these days of general world unrest and of economic stress feelings of tenderness and consideration are so apt to fade within the heart of man. For some really trivial and unworthy reason brothers and sisters become inveterate enemies; elderly parents who have struggled and denied themselves throughout life find, instead of declining years graced with honor, the love and gratitude of their children, only coldness and estrangement. In so many homes, once peaceful and happy, there is disorder, disillusionment, for what was once intended to be the source and crown of perfect joy. More than ever in these disturbing times is there a need for the introduction of forces in the lives of people, dissolving fear, re-establishing simple faith, making for a finer sense of kinship and harmony in our relations with each other.

In the various programs I have produced on the radio I have endeavored to recognize and serve this need. I entered this field when it was not yet out of its "swaddling clothes." Those were the days of crystal sets and "haywire" transmitters, when there was no Federal Communications Commission, when a burst of static was considered an encouraging sign that at last you had succeeded in "tuning in something," when the only programs to bring a human message of any kind were Roxy's Gang and the Happiness Boys. I had entered radio as an announcer after several years of study at a theological seminary and ascended rung by rung as continuity writer, producer, studio manager, etc. With increased experience I developed as a commentator on special events, and as the days went by and my horizon widened I saw radio as a veritable cross section of life, with every broadcasting day a new and glamorous experience, full of exciting possibilities and rich adventure. Here, indeed, was the ideal medium for the promotion of a spirit of tolerance, of peace and brotherhood among people everywhere.

I had always had a lively interest in people, a constant curiosity and a passion for experiencing and observing life. It was quite natural that broadcasts of a human-interest nature should be especially appealing to me. On such broadcasts I received considerable mail. Particularly touching were the letters that came from the afflicted and handicapped in life, the blind, the crippled, the unfortunates who were bedridden, to whom radio was a source of untold blessing. And I tried, while presenting various programs to which I was assigned, to bear in mind particularly this type of listener. In those days most radio speakers, impressed with the possible size of the audience, used a stentorian delivery, or uncertain as they were as to just what was required while speaking in the confines of a cold, forbidding broadcasting studio, addressed the unresponsive steel instrument, more often than not, in a tone obviously stilted or self-conscious. (Few speakers, indeed, had the "radio voices" or the microphone technique that we find among our better commentators and public personalities of this day.) Observing this, I endeavored to speak not to the instrument before me or to a great composite audience that might be tuned in but rather to some sad, lonely person, whom in fancy I pictured listening.

> *Would you have your songs endure?*
> *Build on the human heart.*

I sensed that out there, within that region of silence and darkness, was a great company of souls who did not know each other or see each other, even as I did not know or see them, but who must feel the beat of humanity and who were unified in a common bond by this miraculous instrument.

Much of the mail I received bothered me, for its content was frequently so troubled. There were those in every city and every street, unhappy men and women whose heads were bowed and whose hearts were broken, those who in their anxiety or desperation did not seem to know which way to turn or to whom to go. Apparently they sought to write to someone in whom they felt they could have confidence. Perhaps they would succeed in getting a reply. If not all the information they desired, possibly a word of consolation or encouragement.

That letters of this type were received may be surprising to some, but the reason became increasingly apparent to me. Said this typist or this nurse or this lonely woman or unhappy youth or girl, distracted, desperate: "This is life as I find it; this burden has become too heavy to be borne, the possibilities of life too uncertain to be endured. What may I do? What can I do?" Her friends, her family, her business associates—all have their own desperate needs. More often than not one harassed with personal worries hesitates to share them with those close to her. She fears criticism

or is self-conscious in confiding her mistakes to anyone
whose daily life is linked with hers. So she prefers to pour
her problems into the ears of an absolute stranger, someone
whose work, perhaps, has struck a sympathetic chord,
someone with whom she does not have to be self-conscious.

In any event, not only was I completely without facilities
at that time to answer such letters but, if the truth be told,
was not too sure in every instance of the wise or discreet
answer. But there were inferences to be drawn from these
letters that gave me much concern. Here were bewildered,
groping people, desperately searching for some way out.
These were the vital concerns of society. Yet so little was
being done. It did occur to me, as I listened day after day
to frothy, trifling programs of cheap music and trite, incon-
sequential sketches, that here was radio, great miracle of
our time, reaching intimately into millions of homes. As I
viewed it, here was a remarkable medium expressly con-
ceived for the transmission and reception of sound, con-
quering time and space, concentrating for the most part
on trivia, when it was possible to bring the wealth of the
world's experience and inspiration to the minds and hearts
of the most humble. What contribution could I make? It
will be recalled that in those days even broadcasts of infor-
mation and education, such as interpretive news and stimu-
lating forum discussions, were in the great minority, and
those that existed had achieved no considerable popularity.
I had noticed that many of the problems that had come to
my attention seemed to have a legal angle. I had been un-
favorably impressed with the attempts of professional pur-
veyors of "inspiration" on the radio. Indeed, in moments of
candor more than one admitted to me that most of the an-

swers were of the tongue-in-cheek variety. Restatement of platitudes, glib language, glittering generalities, could accomplish little. What these applicants needed was something much more practical. Either they could or could not find relief from an unhappy social situation usually depending on a particular law that governed it. Since society was not only a sword but a shield, since its purpose was not only to punish but to protect, what remedy did it offer in a given situation as a way out?

My own knowledge of the law was limited to whatever technical reading of a more or less superficial nature I had done, but I had a growing conviction that the law played a far greater part in everyday life than most people ever realized. I knew that ignorance of the law and indifference to it were responsible for much of the regret and misery about us.

I felt that great good could be accomplished by popularizing the law, making it more understandable, that such knowledge would serve as a protection in our association with others. In the final analysis formidable books of statutes and enactments, however technical and forbidding in appearance, are nothing but the codification of the simple rules by which we live, a way of life in which we may walk safely together. I believed, above all, that there existed many unjust laws, that a law was not right because it happened to be a law but because there was right in it, and if there wasn't right in it the quickest way of finding it out was to take it out of the darkness and expose it to the light.

And so, armed with the germ of an idea and given the opportunity to present it by the station with which I was associated—and which, happily, was sympathetic toward the building of a vital human-interest program—I went into New York's famous Night Court, the Magistrates' Courts and the Women's Court. I visited the Family Court and the Children's Court.

It was plain that in many instances, despite the conscientious co-operation of social workers, nothing very much could be done in the way of providing a practical remedy to those seeking redress. This was especially true in the Domestic Relations Court, a sea of confused people. The judges, however well disposed, however touched by the desperate vital concerns of human need, were helpless in the face of certain restrictions of existing law.

Among these unfortunate individuals were to be found creatures reaching in vain for some vestige of hope—victims of desertion, nonsupport, looking quite naturally for some remedy, their husbands in another state and, therefore, technically out of reach or close by in hiding. Sordid tales of merciless beatings, almost unbelievable recitals of wages gambled away, whole families dispossessed and children starved and homeless—these were tragically true stories heard constantly, and yet no way out. If only they could free themselves forever from such heartless, futile existences, bereft of any hope, and start all over again.

And so with the intention of bringing about an enlightened treatment of these and other ills and in the belief that the constructive consideration of such problems would tend toward a better understanding of some of the misadventures that so often plague the community, I convinced many of those in trouble that it might very well be to their interest to relate their problems on the radio anonymously. Their identities would never be revealed. In addition to the advice they might receive, it seemed to me that their experiences and, in particular, the telling of the circumstances that brought them about might chance to divert some otherwise earnest soul listening in from an act which might very well cause a lifetime of misery and sorrow.

I sought and after great difficulty succeeded in obtaining the co-operation of actual judges of our courts, judges of the lower courts, the so-called "people's courts," humane judges who, through contact with the people and their simple problems, could interpret in language stripped of technicality exactly what our rights are under the common law.

Thus it was that there came into being on March 31, 1935, radio's Good Will Court, participated in not by actors but by real people, presided over by actual judges of actual courts, a program with all the elements of education, social benefit, human interest, absorbing drama—full of stark realism and human appeal. There was no script, no rehearsal, always the tense excitement of the unexpected. By the use of voice filters and the withholding of names I was able to preserve the anonymity of those who appeared.

It would seem that no aspect of human living was foreign to this experience. In following up cases I journeyed to the cold, gray walls of our institutions for the poor, the barred windows of our prisons, the uninviting entrances of our asylums. I have seen sorrowing mothers and fathers, bowed down with such grief, that I wondered if it were possible for human love to make so great a sacrifice and yet not die.

Lest it be mistakenly assumed that the people dealt with were in no sense average but rather the dregs at the bottom of the social cup, it should be stated that such was not the case. While there was a certain percentage of chronic invalids of our economic world, this class did not constitute the major part of those with whom I dealt. It was obvious that a substantial number were wellborn, decently brought up, of at least average education, but in so many instances had been victims of the economic depression. Involved in some hopeless entanglement and unable to find a way out, they swallowed their pride and came.

Gradually the full significance of the Good Will Court, its social meaning and importance, sank into the public consciousness, and after a few months it became radio's greatest "sensation." The response from the listening audience was without precedent in broadcasting. It reigned as a top-ranking radio feature for two years, uncovering issues that went to the heart of injustices and inequalities in the law and the rights of citizens in a democratic nation. It dealt with the most trifling of matters to the most vital and desperate that could possibly affect the lives of human beings. The spotlight of public attention placed on these distressing situations served as a constructive example to countless listeners-in, tended to diminish the possibility of their recurrence, exposed artifices and rackets, served to reduce some of the unhappiness that exists about us. Important government officials, social agencies, the press and public shared this view. But there were forces at work busily undermining that which was being done, those who misunderstood or chose to misunderstand the Good Will Court's intent and purpose.

For two years some sixty distinguished judges of our duly constituted courts had given of their time and energy, obviously because they believed something significant was being accomplished in the direction of public education.

Introduction

Early one morning I was awakened by a telephone call
from an executive of the Associated Press who read to my
stunned ears a legal ruling making it technically impossible
to have these judges continue to advise on the grounds of
"legal ethics." We had thought it important to aid distressed
people in a practical way. It had been felt that if "igno-
rance of the law is no excuse," there was an obligation on the
part of society to advise people as to their rights or absence
of rights in a given situation. From the point of view of
many, to shut off this method of speech, this medium of
education and this incitement to public thinking was a gross
interference with the freedom of speech and of thought. To
do so purely on technical and legalistic grounds and for the
fancied benefit of some particular class would seem to deny
fundamental rights and restrict the liberties and opportuni-
ties of the whole community. But there could be no appeal
from the arbitrary decision. This work was finished. The
tens of thousands of protests and petitions from the audi-
ence of millions of dismayed listeners were of no avail.

As was inevitable, the pattern having been established,
imitations on other stations throughout the country grew up
like mushrooms. The original name even and program for-
mula were closely approximated for programs of "Confes-
sion" and "Advice."

For months I was the most restless man in New York. I
was convinced that something true and good had been
killed. It was suggested that I dramatize some of the situ-
ations that had come to my attention and present them in
such a way as to accomplish the same result. The idea of
promoting social and legal reform through the drama and
other literary productions was not new. It is well known

that the laws of England were in many respects liberalized by Dickens, touching as he did upon the underprivileged classes in his literary portrayal of the actual workings of the law and the injustices of its administration. Indeed, such a method has always been a widely recognized means to social progress. The material I had in my possession was invaluable. I produced and presented to a nationwide audience the Court of Human Relations, also known as A. L. Alexander's True Story Court.

In February 1937 there was first devised the Mediation Program (There Are Two Sides to Every Story called as well "The Court of Human Relations"), and this has since occupied my attention. The principle wherein two persons having a matter of difference may submit the issue for hearing and settlement to a third party or board was a radio "natural." It grows out of man's instinct to administer justice and his passion for fair play in human relations. It was existent when man emerged from the animal state several hundred thousand years before the cave man. Indeed, it is a principle so old that it is lost in antiquity.

In this world, so concerned with the elemental struggle for existence, tensions and animosities among us do arise. Where there is a partnership, whether it be in our personal relations or in business, there is often discord, and persons who enter into an arrangement of any kind, notwithstanding every friendly feeling they may have toward each other at the time, realize that differences may come between them. To enter into mediation is to engage in a simple and direct means of determining what is just and right and fair in a given situation, without technicality and red tape.

The object of the Mediation Program is to educate the

public to the existence of a method by which grievances, when submitted to a board and approached tolerantly and sympathetically, can be heard and settled with a minimum of delay, with justice, with impartiality and, in most cases, with finality. The Mediation Board's permanent panel is made up of over one hundred distinguished citizens, public officials, industrialists, clergymen, authors and educators. The three presiding at a given broadcast are selected from this panel of key personalities in American life.

The men and women who appear before the board, while basically interested in settling their own controversies, have the wistful idea that their issues are the issues of millions of others as well. In the presentation of such a feature, there is the conviction that if consideration is given to attitudes of mind which interfere with peace and happiness, thought may be set in motion and there may be revealed certain principles of truth, which when applied "are the solution of all issues and the healing of all ills."

Whatever any or all of these broadcasts had or did not have, there was one feature common to all of them. Each had the capacity to start the community thinking and thereby prepare the ground for the advancement of progress. Because of their realism and human interest they touched the heart and often inspired the desire for reformation. All were related in the sense that they grew out of the same basic purpose and human need.

There was one other feature common to all of these programs, the custom of concluding each of them with an appropriate poem. I have always had the conviction that poetry of a human and simple nature satisfies a hunger that is part of nearly every person's make-up. Such expression served to point up and summarize what had been said in a more general way on the program proper, and I found it the most gracious and effective way of bringing the hour to a natural and logical conclusion.

The first time I tried this a broadcast executive told me quite bluntly that it tended to spoil the program. "What on earth is poetry good for anyway?" he asked, just as editors so often have. The answer is found in stacks of mail—requests for copies of some favorite of the listener. Tens of thousands of people in every conceivable walk of life have continued to write, have seemed to be lifted up by a simple verse having the capacity to inspire patience of heart or rekindle hope and faith. While some of the poems brought barely a ripple of response in comparison with others, I soon found the elements necessary in order to appeal to the feelings and arouse the imagination of the listener.

From countless listeners-in came insistent requests that these poems be included in a single volume. Of the many hundreds read on the air I have included only those which aroused the warmest and most enthusiastic response—each one a classic of human appeal.

And so I have a direct answer to the question: "What on earth is poetry good for anyway?" In a restless world it shows that certain ways of living are better than certain other ways, ways that may enrich and beautify and strengthen our lives. In a world inhabited by a human family forever in conflict, selfish, disintegrated, fomenting prejudice and hate, it emphasizes those elements in life which complement each other rather than contradict each other, which bring people together rather than separate and divide. In a world obsessed by fear it helps us to learn to bear everyday trials and annoyances gently and calmly, teaches us there can be no inward peace or happiness without some elemental faith in life's essential goodness. Such are "the things that poetry is good for."

Some noble spirit once said, "The books of theologians gather dust upon my shelves, but the pages of the poets are stained with my fingers and blotted with my tears." Here are reprinted not only the "poetic greats" but, as well, a number of little-known poets who "shot an arrow into the air." I am especially happy to be able to treasure in these pages some of the gems of "the little poets fame forgot."

To all the poets, great and small, whose kind permission to use their work made this unique volume possible, my humble thanks. For those who cannot speak for themselves, they speak, and it is as if we have spoken. Daring to dream "beyond the lean horizon of their days," they have opened up a world of affections and loyalties, of visions and ideals, of devotion and sacrifice. As Browning said of the Emperor Justinian's digest of the old Roman laws, the poets here

> *made precise*
> *What simply sparkled in men's eyes before,*
> *Twitched in their brow or quivered on their lip,*
> *Waited the speech they called but would not come.*

They deal here with man and the hopes of his soul, man struggling with his destiny. Shelley called poets such as these "the unacknowledged legislators of the world." Surely if wars and greed and strife are one day to be no more, it will not be because of legislators but rather because of the poets who conspire to mold the sorry scheme of things "nearer to the heart's desire."

A. L. ALEXANDER

Poems That Touch The Heart

AROUND THE CORNER

Around the corner I have a friend,
In this great city that has no end;
Yet days go by, and weeks rush on,
And before I know it a year is gone,
And I never see my old friend's face,
For Life is a swift and terrible race.
He knows I like him just as well
As in the days when I rang his bell
And he rang mine. We were younger then,
And now we are busy, tired men:
Tired with playing a foolish game,
Tired with trying to make a name.
"Tomorrow," I say, "I will call on Jim,
Just to show that I'm thinking of him."
But tomorrow comes—and tomorrow goes,
And the distance between us grows and grows
Around the corner!—yet miles away. . . .
"Here's a telegram, sir. . . ."
                    "Jim died today."
And that's what we get, and deserve in the end:
Around the corner, a vanished friend.

                                CHARLES HANSON TOWNE

A poem or a verse may be said to be worth while when it finds its way into the special crevice of a person's need. Most of us want a quiet, peaceful life. The word generally used to describe this is—*"Security"*—a state of well-being, of freedom from irksome care, from danger, from anxiety. However, when devotion to security is carried too far, it becomes a vice that stunts the personality. To avoid anything that is new and different, unless success is absolutely assured, prevents us from making full use of our potentialities.

Unless we are willing to take a chance on the unknown, our horizon becomes narrowed, our ambition stifled, and there can be no progress. The person adventurous enough to take a chance is putting his enthusiasms to work. Without enthusiasm there can be no fruit of enjoyment.

Granted the goal desired is truly wise, is really worth fighting for, a verse having the capacity to inspire can impel us to persevering action.

SUCCESS

If you want a thing bad enough
To go out and fight for it,
Work day and night for it,
Give up your time and your peace and your sleep for it
If only desire of it
Makes you quite mad enough
Never to tire of it,
Makes you hold all other things tawdry and cheap for it
If life seems all empty and useless without it
And all that you scheme and you dream is about it,
If gladly you'll sweat for it,

Fret for it,
Plan for it,
Lose all your terror of God or man for it,
If you'll simply go after that thing that you want,
With all your capacity,
Strength and sagacity,
Faith, hope and confidence, stern pertinacity,
If neither cold poverty, famished and gaunt,
Nor sickness nor pain
Of body or brain
Can turn you away from the thing that you want,
If dogged and grim you besiege and beset it,
                    You'll get it!

                                        BERTON BRALEY

One hour of life, crowded to the full with glorious action,
and filled with noble risks, is worth whole years of those
mean observances of paltry decorum in which men steal
through existence like sluggish waters through a marsh,
without either honor or observation.

                                        SIR WALTER SCOTT

WHY DO I LOVE YOU?

I love you,
Not only for what you are,
But for what I am
When I am with you.

I love you
Not only for what
You have made of yourself,
But for what
You are making of me.

I love you
For ignoring the possibilities
Of the fool in me
And for laying firm hold
Of the possibilities for good.

Why do I love you?

I love you
For closing your eyes
To the discords—
And for adding to the music in me
By worshipful listening.

I love you because you
Are helping me to make
Of the lumber of my life
Not a tavern
But a temple;
And out of the words
Of my every day
Not a reproach
But a song.

I love you
Because you have done
More than any creed
To make me happy.

You have done it
Without a word,
Without a touch,
Without a sign.
You have done it
Just by being yourself.

After all
Perhaps that is what
Love means.

ROY CROFT

THE DARK CANDLE

A man had a little daughter—an only and much-beloved child. He lived for her—she was his life. So when she became ill and her illness resisted the efforts of the best obtainable physicians, he became like a man possessed, moving heaven and earth to bring about her restoration to health.

His best efforts proved unavailing and the child died. The father was totally irreconcilable. He became a bitter recluse, shutting himself away from his many friends and refusing every activity that might restore his poise and bring him back to his normal self.

But one night he had a dream. He was in Heaven, and was witnessing a grand pageant of all the little child angels. They were marching in an apparently endless line past the Great White Throne. Every white-robed angelic tot carried a candle. He noticed that one child's candle was not lighted. Then he saw that the child with the dark candle was his own little girl. Rushing to her, while the pageant faltered, he seized her in his arms, caressed her tenderly, and then asked:

"How is it, darling, that your candle alone is unlighted?"

"Father, they often relight it, but your tears always put it out."

Just then he awoke from his dream. The lesson was crystal clear, and its effects were immediate. From that hour on he was not a recluse, but mingled freely and cheerfully with his former friends and associates. No longer would his little darling's candle be extinguished by his useless tears!

STRICKLAND GILLILAN

A FRIEND

What is a Friend? I'll tell you.
It is a person with whom you dare to be yourself.
Your soul can go naked with him.

He seems to ask you to put on nothing, only to be what you really are.

When you are with him, you do not have to be on your guard.

You can say what you think, so long as it is genuinely you.

He understands those contradictions in your nature that cause others to misjudge you.

With him you breathe freely—you can avow your little vanities and envies and absurdities and in opening them up to him they are dissolved on the white ocean of his loyalty.

He understands.—You can weep with him, laugh with him, pray with him—through and underneath it all he sees, knows and loves you.

A Friend, I repeat, is one with whom YOU DARE TO BE YOUR-SELF.

AUTHOR UNKNOWN

WHAT IS YOUTH?

Youth is not a time of life, it is a state of mind. It is not a matter of ripe cheeks, red lips, supple knees; it is a temper of the will, a quality of the imagination, a vigor of the emotions; it is a freshness of the deep springs of life. Youth means a temperamental predominance of courage over timidity, of the appetite of adventure over the love of ease. This often exists in a man of fifty more than a boy of twenty. Nobody grows old merely by living a number of years; people grow old only by deserting their ideals. Years may wrinkle the skin, but to give up enthusiasm wrinkles the soul.

Worry, doubt, self-distrust, fear and despair, these are the long, long years that bow the head and turn the growing spirit back to dust. Whether seventy or seventeen there is in every being's heart the love of wonder, the sweet amazement of the stars and starlight things and thoughts, the undaunted challenge of events, the unfailing child-like appetite for what is next, and the joy and the game of life.

You are as young as your faith, as old as your doubt; as young as your self-confidence, as old as your fear; as young as your hope, as old as your despair.

In the central place of your heart there is a sensitive station. So long as it receives messages of beauty, hope, cheer, grandeur, courage and power from the earth, from men and from the Infinite, so long are you young.

AUTHOR UNKNOWN

SHOULD YOU GO FIRST

Should you go first and I remain
   To walk the road alone,
I'll live in memory's garden, dear,
   With happy days we've known.
In Spring I'll watch for roses red
   When fades the lilac blue,
In early Fall when brown leaves call
   I'll catch a glimpse of you.

8

Should you go first and I remain
    For battles to be fought,
Each thing you've touched along the way
    Will be a hallowed spot.
I'll hear your voice, I'll see your smile,
    Though blindly I may grope,
The memory of your helping hand
    Will buoy me on with hope.

Should you go first and I remain
    To finish with the scroll,
No length'ning shadows shall creep in
    To make this life seem droll.
We've known so much of happiness,
    We've had our cup of joy
And memory is one gift of God
    That death cannot destroy.

Should you go first and I remain,
    One thing I'd have you do;
Walk slowly down that long, lone path,
    For soon I'll follow you.
I'll want to know each step you take
    That I may walk the same.
For someday, down that lonely road,
    You'll hear me call your name.

ALBERT ROWSWELL

There is no power of love so hard to get and keep as a kind voice. Watch it day by day as a pearl of great price, for it is worth more than the finest pearl hid in the sea. A kind voice is to the heart like light is to the eye. It is a light that sings as well as shines.

THE TONE OF VOICE

It's not so much what you say
As the manner in which you say it;
It's not so much the language you use
As the tone in which you convey it;
"Come here!" I sharply said,
And the child cowered and wept.
"Come here," I said—
He looked and smiled
And straight to my lap he crept.
Words may be mild and fair
And the tone may pierce like a dart;
Words may be soft as the summer air
But the tone may break my heart;
For words come from the mind
Grow by study and art—
But tone leaps from the inner self
Revealing the state of the heart.
Whether you know it or not,

Whether you mean or care,
Gentleness, kindness, love, and hate,
Envy, anger, are there.
Then, would you quarrels avoid
And peace and love rejoice?
Keep anger not only out of your words—
Keep it out of your voice.

AUTHOR UNKNOWN

TREASURES

His overalls hung on the hook by his hat, and I noticed
    his pockets were bulging out fat.
So I emptied them out in a pile on the chair, and I tenderly
    touched ev'ry treasure with care:

There were three rubber bands, a parking lot ticket,
Two paper clips and a fishing cricket,
A camphor ball and an empty match box,
A half dozen nails and a couple of rocks,
A yellow golf tee, two lollypop sticks,
A marble, a spool and three tooth picks,
A knife and a pencil, some dry corn silk,
A wire and a cap from a bottle of milk,
A rusty door key and a white chicken feather,
An old clock gear and a piece of leather,
A flash-light bulb and three or four strings,
A broken dog biscuit and two hair springs.

Then I gathered them up, all his "treasures" so grand—
   ev'ry rock, ev'ry nail and each rubber band,
And I put them all back, then I kissed him good-night,
   and he smiled in his sleep as I turned out the light.
And I thrilled as I thought of the fun and the joy such
   trivial things could give to a boy.

CLAIRE RICHCREEK THOMAS

Many men know the laws of mathematics and are skilled in the arts, but most men know very little about the laws governing life, the art of living. One may be able to build an airplane and circle the globe and yet be entirely ignorant of the simple art of how to be happy, successful, and content. When studying the arts, place first upon the list *the art of living.*

AUTHOR UNKNOWN

TELL HER SO

Amid the cares of married strife
   In spite of toil and business life
If you value your dear wife—
   Tell her so!

When days are dark and deeply blue
   She has her troubles, same as you
Show her that your love is true
   Tell her so!

Don't act as if she's past her prime
  As tho' to please her were a crime
If ever you loved her, now's the time—
  Tell her so!

She'll return for each caress
  A hundred fold of tenderness,
Hearts like hers were made to bless;
  Tell her so!

You are hers and hers alone;
  Well you know she's all your own;
Don't wait to carve it on a stone—
  Tell her so!

Never let her heart grow cold
  Richer beauties will unfold
She is worth her weight in gold
  Tell her so!

                AUTHOR UNKNOWN

HAPPINESS

Happiness is like a crystal,
Fair and exquisite and clear,
Broken in a million pieces,
Shattered, scattered far and near.
Now and then along life's pathway,
Lo! some shining fragments fall;
But there are so many pieces
No one ever finds them all.

You may find a bit of beauty,
Or an honest share of wealth,
While another just beside you
Gathers honor, love or health.
Vain to choose or grasp unduly,
Broken is the perfect ball,
And there are so many pieces,
No one ever finds them all.

Yet the wise as on they journey
Treasure every fragment clear,
Fit them as they may together,
Imaging the shattered sphere,
Learning ever to be thankful,
Though their share of it is small;
For it has so many pieces
No one ever finds them all.

PRISCILLA LEONARD

GOODNIGHT
(For Husbands and Wives)

This day is almost done. When the night and morning meet it will be only an unalterable memory. So let no unkind word; no careless, doubting thought; no guilty secret; no neglected duty; no wisp of jealous fog becloud its passing . . .

Now, as we put our arms around each other, in sincere and affectionate token of our deep and abiding love, we would lay aside all disturbing thoughts, all misunderstandings, all unworthiness . . . Who is to blame is not important; only how shall we set the situation right. And so, serving and being served, loving and being loved, blessing and being blessed, we shall make a happy, peaceful home, where hearts shall never drop their leaves, but where we and our children shall learn to face life joyfully, fearlessly, triumphantly, so near as God shall give us grace.

Goodnight, beloved.

F. ALEXANDER MAGOUN

THE LITTLE CHAP WHO FOLLOWS ME

A careful man I ought to be;
A little fellow follows me;
I do not dare to go astray
For fear he'll go the self-same way.

I must not madly step aside,
Where pleasure's paths are smooth and wide,
And join in wine's red revelry—
A little fellow follows me.

I cannot once escape his eyes:
Whate'er he sees me do he tries—
Like me, he says, he's going to be;
The little chap who follows me.

He thinks that I am good and fine,
Believes in every word of mine;
The base in me he must not see,
The little chap who follows me.

I must remember as I go,
Through summer's sun and winter's snow,
I'm building for the years to be,
A little fellow follows me.

                                                    AUTHOR UNKNOWN

HOW DO I LOVE THEE?

How do I love thee? Let me count the ways.
I love thee to the depth and breadth and height
My soul can reach, when feeling out of sight
For the ends of Being and ideal Grace.
I love thee to the level of everyday's
Most quiet need, by sun and candle-light.
I love thee freely, as men strive for Right;
I love thee purely, as they turn from Praise.
I love thee with the passion put to use
In my old griefs, and with my childhood's faith.
I love thee with a love I seemed to lose
With my lost saints,—I love thee with the breath,
Smiles, tears, of all my life!—and, if God choose,
I shall but love thee better after death.

                                        ELIZABETH BARRETT BROWNING

THE STORY OF LIFE

Say! what is life? 'Tis to be born
  A hapless babe; to greet the light
With a sharp wail, as if the morn
  Foretold a cloudy morn and night;
To weep, to sleep and weep again,
With sunny smiles between; and then;—

And then apace the infant grows
  To be a laughing, sprightly boy,
Happy despite his little woes;
  Were he but conscious of his joy,
To be, in short, from two to ten,
A merry, moody child; and then;—

And then, in coat and trousers clad,
  To learn to say the decalogue;
And break it—an unthinking lad,
  With mirth and mischief all agog,
A truant oft; by field and fen
To capture butterflies; and then;—

And then, increased in strength and size,
  To be anon, a youth, full grown,
A hero in his mother's eyes;
  A young Apollo in his own,
To imitate the ways of men
In fashionable sins; and then;—

And then, at last, to be a man;
To fall in love, to woo, to wed;
With seething brain to scheme and plan;
To gather gold, or toil for bread;
To sue for fame, with tongue or pen;
To gain or lose the prize; and then;—

And then in gray and wrinkled eld,
To mourn the speed of life's decline;
To praise the scenes his youth beheld,
And dwell in memory of Lang Syne;
To dream awhile with darkened ken,
Then drop into his grave; *and then;—*

JOHN G. SAXE

ALABASTER BOXES

Do not keep the alabaster boxes of your love and tenderness sealed up, until your friends are dead. Fill their lives with sweetness. Speak approving, cheering words while their ears can hear them and while their hearts can be thrilled and made happier by them. The kind things you mean to say when they are gone, say them before they go. The flowers you mean to send—use to brighten and sweeten their homes before they leave them. If my friends have alabaster boxes laid away, full of fragrant perfumes of sympathy and affection I would rather they would bring them out in my weary and troubled hours and open them, that I may be refreshed and cheered when I need them. Let us

learn to anoint our friends beforehand. Post-mortem kind-
nesses do not cheer the burdened spirit. Flowers cast no
fragrance backward over the weary way.

AUTHOR UNKNOWN

THE TOUCH OF THE MASTER'S HAND

'Twas battered and scarred, and the auctioneer
Thought it scarcely worth his while
To waste much time on the old violin,
But held it up with a smile.
"What am I bidden, good folks," he cried,
"Who will start bidding for me?
A dollar, a dollar"—then, "Two!" "Only two?
Two dollars, and who'll make it three?
Three dollars once; three dollars, twice;
Going for three—" But no,
From the room, far back, a gray-haired man
Came forward and picked up the bow;
Then, wiping the dust from the old violin,
And tightening the loose strings,
He played a melody pure and sweet
As sweet as a caroling angel sings.

The music ceased, and the auctioneer,
With a voice that was quiet and low,
Said, "What am I bidden for the old violin?"
And he held it up with the bow.
"A thousand dollars, and who'll make it two?
Two thousand! And who'll make it three?

Three thousand, once; three thousand, twice;
And going, and gone!" said he.
The people cheered, but some of them cried,
"We do not quite understand
What changed its worth?" Swift came the reply:
"The touch of the master's hand."

And many a man with life out of tune,
And battered and scattered with sin,
Is auctioned cheap to the thoughtless crowd,
Much like the old violin.
A "mess of pottage," a glass of wine;
A game—and he travels on.
He's "going" once, and "going" twice,
He's "going" and almost "gone."
But the Master comes, and the foolish crowd
Never can quite understand
The worth of a soul, and the change that's wrought
By the touch of the Master's hand.

MYRA BROOKS WELCH

ON CHILDREN

. . . Your children are not your children.
They are the sons and daughters of Life's longing for itself.
They come through you but not from you,
And though they are with you yet they belong not to you.
You may give them your love but not your thoughts.
For they have their own thoughts.

You may house their bodies but not their souls,
For their souls dwell in the house of tomorrow, which you
  cannot visit, not even in your dreams.
You may strive to be like them, but seek not to make them
  like you.
For life goes not backward nor tarries with yesterday . . .

FROM *The Prophet* BY KAHLIL GIBRAN

THE BAR

The Saloon is sometimes called a Bar,
  A Bar to heaven, a door to hell
Whoever named it, named it well;
  A Bar to manliness and wealth
A door to want and broken health;
  A Bar to honor, pride and fame
A door to grief and sin and shame;
  A Bar to hope, a bar to prayer
A door to darkness and despair;
  A Bar to honored useful life
A door to brawling, senseless strife;
  A Bar to all that's true and brave
A door to every drunkard's grave;
  A Bar to joys that home imparts
A door to tears and aching hearts;
  A Bar to heaven, a door to hell
Whoever named it, named it well!

By a convict serving a life term in Joliet Prison, Illinois.

YOUR HOUSE

The walls of a house are not built of wood, brick or stone, but of truth and loyalty.

Unpleasant sounds of grumbling, the friction of living, the clash of personalities, are not deadened by Persian rugs or polished floors, but by conciliation, and concession. . . .

The house is not a structure where bodies meet, but a hearthstone upon which flames mingle, separate flames of souls, which, the more perfectly they unite, the more clearly they shine and the straighter they rise toward heaven.

Your house is your fortress in a warring world, where a woman's hand buckles on your armor in the morning and soothes your fatigue and wounds at night.

The beauty of a house is harmony.

The security of a house is loyalty.

The joy of a house is love.

The plenty of a house is in children.

The rule of a house is service.

The comfort of a house is in contented spirits.

The maker of a house, of a real human house, is God himself, the same who made the stars and built the world.

AUTHOR UNKNOWN

THE HAPPIEST SEASON

The question, "Which is the happiest season of life," being referred to an aged man, he replied: "When spring comes, and in the soft air the buds are breaking on the trees, and they are covered with blossoms, I think, 'How beautiful is Spring!' And when the summer comes, and covers the trees with its heavy foliage, and singing birds are among the branches, I think, 'How beautiful is Summer!' When autumn loads them with golden fruit, and their leaves bear the gorgeous tint of frost, I think, 'How beautiful is Autumn!' And when it is sere winter, and there is neither foliage nor fruit, then I look up through the leafless branches, as I never could until now, *and see the stars shine.*"

AUTHOR UNKNOWN

Be not too wise, nor too foolish,
Be not too conceited, nor diffident,
Be not too haughty, nor too humble,
Be not too talkative, nor too silent,
Be not too hard, nor too feeble.
If you be too wise, men will expect too much of you;
If you be too foolish, you will be deceived;
If you be too conceited, you will be thought difficult;
If you be too humble, you will be without honour;
If you be too talkative, you will not be heeded;

If you be too silent, you will not be regarded;
If you be too hard, you will be broken;
If you be too feeble, you will be crushed.

INSTRUCTIONS OF KING CORMAC
KING OF CASHEL (IRISH, NINTH CENTURY)

The day began with dismal doubt
A stubborn thing to put to rout;
But all my worries flew away
When someone smiled at me today.

AUTHOR UNKNOWN

AT SET OF SUN

If you sit down at set of sun
And count the acts that you have done,
    And, counting, find
One self-denying deed, one word
That eased the heart of him who heard—
    One glance most kind,
That fell like sunshine where it went—
Then you may count that day well spent.

But, if, through all the livelong day,
You've cheered no heart, by yea or nay—
    If, through it all

You've nothing done that you can trace
That brought the sunshine to one face—
    No act most small
That helped some soul and nothing cost—
Then count that day as worse than lost.

                          GEORGE ELIOT

They might not need me; but they might.
I'll let my head be just in sight;
A smile as small as mine might be
Precisely their necessity.

                          EMILY DICKINSON

A PRAYER FOUND IN CHESTER
CATHEDRAL

Give me a good digestion, Lord,
And also something to digest;
Give me a healthy body, Lord,
With sense to keep it at its best.

Give me a healthy mind, good Lord,
To keep the good and pure in sight;
Which, seeing sin, is not appalled,
But finds a way to set it right.

Give me a mind that is not bored,
That does not whimper, whine or sigh;
Don't let me worry overmuch
About the fussy thing called "I".

Give me a sense of humor, Lord,
Give me the grace to see a joke;
To get some happiness from life,
And pass it on to other folk.

THE SCULPTOR

I took a piece of plastic clay
And idly fashioned it one day,
And as my fingers pressed it, still
It bent and yielded to my will.

I came again, when days were passed,
The bit of clay was hard at last,
The form I gave it, still it bore,
But I could change that form no more.

Then I took a piece of *living* clay
And gently formed it, day by day
And molded with my power and art,
A young child's soft and yielding heart.

I came again when years were gone,
It was a *man* I looked upon.
He still that early impress bore,
And I could change it, nevermore.

AUTHOR UNKNOWN

Bless the four corners of this house,
And be the doorway blest; its nooks, its sun,
Its rooms, its chambers every one.

DREAM HOUSE

Let there be within these phantom walls
Beauty where the hearth fire's shadow falls . . .
Quiet pictures—books—and welcoming chairs . . .
Music that the very silence shares . . .
Kitchen windows curtained blue and white . . .
Shelves and cupboards built for my delight . . .
Little things that lure and beckon me
With their tranquil joy! And let there be
Lilt of laughter—swift-forgotten tears
Woven through the fabric of the years . . .
Strength to guard me—eyes to answer mine,
Mutely clear. And though without may shine
Stars of dawn or sunset's wistful glow—
All of life and love my house shall know!

CATHERINE PARMENTER NEWELL

THE WORLD NEEDS

A little more kindness and a little less creed,
A little more giving and a little less greed;
A little more smile and a little less frown,
A little less kicking a man when he's down;
A little more "we" and a little less "I,"
A little more laugh and a little less cry;
A few more flowers on the pathway of life,
And fewer on graves at the end of the strife.

AUTHOR UNKNOWN

WIDE WALLS

Give me wide walls to build my house of Life—
The North shall be of Love, against the winds of fate;
The South of Tolerance, that I may outreach hate;
The East of Faith, that rises clear and new each day;
The West of Hope, that e'en dies a glorious way.
The threshold 'neath my feet shall be Humility;
The roof—the very sky itself—Infinity.
Give me wide walls to build my house of Life.

AUTHOR UNKNOWN

MISS YOU

I miss you in the morning, dear,
 When all the world is new;
I know the day can bring no joy
 Because it brings not you.
I miss the well-loved voice of you,
 Your tender smile for me,
The charm of you, the joy of your
 Unfailing sympathy.

The world is full of folks, it's true,
 But there was only one of you.

I miss you at the noontide, dear;
 The crowded city street
Seems but a desert now, I walk
 In solitude complete.
I miss your hand beside my own
 The light touch of your hand,
The quick gleam in the eyes of you
 So sure to understand.

The world is full of folks, it's true,
 But there was only one of you.

I miss you in the evening, dear,
  When daylight fades away;
I miss the sheltering arms of you
  To rest me from the day,
I try to think I see you yet
  There where the firelight gleams—
Weary at last, I sleep, and still
  I miss you in my dreams.

THE WORLD IS FULL OF FOLKS, IT'S TRUE,
BUT THERE WAS ONLY ONE OF YOU.

AUTHOR UNKNOWN

THE MEANING OF A LETTER

Messenger of Sympathy and Love
Servant of Parted Friends
Consoler of the Lonely
Bond of the Scattered Family
Enlarger of the Common Life
Carrier of News and Knowledge
Instrument of Trade and Industry
Promoter of Mutual Acquaintance
Of Peace and Good Will

INSCRIBED ON THE UNITED STATES
POST OFFICE IN WASHINGTON, D.C.

BANKRUPT

One midnight, deep in starlight still,
I dreamed that I received this bill:
(- - - - IN ACCOUNT WITH LIFE - - - -):
Five thousand breathless dawns all new;
Five thousand flowers fresh in dew;
Five thousand sunsets wrapped in gold;
One-million snow-flakes served ice-cold;
Five quiet friends; one baby's love;
One white-mad sea with clouds above;
One hundred music-haunted dreams
Of moon-drenched roads and hurrying streams;
Of prophesying winds, and trees;
Of silent stars and browsing bees;
One June night in a fragrant wood;
One heart that loved and understood.
I wondered when I waked at day,
How—how in God's name—I could pay!

CORTLANDT W. SAYRES

A BAG OF TOOLS

Isn't it strange
That princes and kings,
And clowns that caper
In sawdust rings,

And common people
Like you and me
Are builders for eternity?

Each is given a bag of tools,
A shapeless mass,
A book of rules;
And each must make—
Ere life is flown—
A stumbling block
Or a steppingstone.

R. L. SHARPE

During the more than half century since "A Last Will" was first published by *Harper's Weekly* it has been reprinted countless times in newspapers, magazines, anthologies—variously titled, sometimes considerably shortened, other times appended, almost always drastically changed, and seldom giving proper credit to its author—Williston Fish, a successful businessman who wrote *A Last Will* in 1897. The original Charles Lounsbury was a name in the author's family several generations earlier, but the will itself is a product of Mr. Fish's imagination, as well as his convictions as to life's most cherished values.

A LAST WILL

I, Charles Lounsbury, being of sound and disposing mind and memory, do now make and publish this my last will and testament, in order, as justly as I may, to distribute my interests in the world among succeeding men.

32

And first, that part of my interests which is known among men and recognized in the sheep-bound volumes of the law as my property, being inconsiderable and of no account, I make no disposition of in this my will.

My right to live, being but a life estate, is not at my disposal, but, these things excepted, all else in the world I now proceed to devise and bequeath.

ITEM: I give to good fathers and mothers, in trust for their children, all good little words of praise and encouragement and all quaint pet names and endearments; and I charge said parents to use them justly, but generously, as the needs of their children shall require.

ITEM: I leave to children inclusively, but only for the term of their childhood, all, and every, the flowers of the field, and the blossoms of the woods, with the right to play among them freely according to the custom of children, warning them at the same time against the thistles and the thorns. And I devise to the children, the banks of the brooks and the golden sands beneath the waters thereof, and the odors of the willows that dip therein, and the white clouds that float high over the giant trees.

And I leave the children the long, long days to be merry in, in a thousand ways, and the night and the moon and the train of the Milky Way to wonder at, but subject, nevertheless, to the rights hereinafter given to lovers.

ITEM: I devise to boys, jointly, all the idle fields and commons where ball may be played, all pleasant waters where one may swim, all snow-clad hills where one may coast, and all streams and ponds where one may fish, or where, when grim winter comes, one may skate, to have and to hold the same for the period of their boyhood. And all meadows, with the clover-blossoms and butterflies thereof; the woods with their appurtenances; the squirrels and birds and echoes and strange noises, and all distant places, which may be visited, together with the adventures there to be found. And I give to said boys each his own place at the fireside at night, with all pictures that may be seen in the burning wood, to enjoy without hindrance and without any incumbrance of care.

ITEM: To lovers, I devise their imaginary world, with whatever they may need, as the stars of the sky, the red, red roses by the wall, the snow of the hawthorn, the sweet strains of music, and aught else they may desire to figure to each other the lastingness and beauty of their love.

ITEM: To young men jointly, being joined in a brave mad crowd, I devise and bequeath all boisterous, inspiring sports of rivalry, I give to them the disdain of weakness and un-daunted confidence in their own strength. Though they are rude and rough, I leave to them alone the power of making lasting friendships and of possessing companions, and to them exclusively I give all merry songs and brave choruses to sing with lusty voices.

ITEM: And to those who are no longer children, or youths, or lovers, I leave Memory, and I bequeath to them the volumes of the poems of Burns and Shakespeare, and of other poets, if there are others, to the end that they may live the old days over again freely and fully, without tithe or diminution.

ITEM: To the loved ones with snowy crowns, I bequeath the happiness of old age, the love and gratitude of their children until they fall asleep.

YOU MUSTN'T QUIT

It was James J. Corbett, former heavyweight champion of the world who said: "Fight one more round." When your feet are so tired that you have to shuffle back to the center of the ring, fight one more round! *When your arms are so tired that you can hardly lift your hands to come on guard,* fight one more round! *When your nose is bleeding and your eyes are black and you're so tired that you wish your opponent would crack you one on the jaw and put you to sleep—* DON'T QUIT—FIGHT ONE MORE ROUND.

When things go wrong, as they sometimes will,
When the road you're trudging seems all uphill,
When the funds are low and the debts are high
And you want to smile, but you have to sigh,
When care is pressing you down a bit,
Rest! if you must—but never quit.

Life is queer, with its twists and turns,
As every one of us sometimes learns,
And many a failure turns about
When he might have won if he'd stuck it out;
Stick to your task, though the pace seems slow—
You may succeed with one more blow.

Success is failure turned inside out—
The silver tint of the clouds of doubt—
And you never can tell how close you are,
It may be near when it seems afar;
So stick to the fight when you're hardest hit—
It's when things seem worst that YOU MUSTN'T QUIT.

AUTHOR UNKNOWN

HOME IS WHERE THERE'S ONE TO LOVE US

Home's not merely four square walls,
    Though with pictures hung and gilded;
Home is where Affection calls,
    Filled with shrines the Heart hath builded!
Home!—go watch the faithful dove,
    Sailing 'neath the heaven above us;
Home is where there's one to love!
    Home is where there's one to love us!

Home's not merely roof and room—
    It needs something to endear it;
Home is where the heart can bloom,
    Where there's some kind lip to cheer it!

What is home with none to meet,
　None to welcome, none to greet us?
Home is sweet—and only sweet—
　Where there's one we love to meet us!

CHARLES SWAIN

WELCOME OVER THE DOOR OF AN OLD INN

Hail, Guest! We ask not what thou art;
If Friend, we greet thee, hand and heart;
If Stranger, such no longer be;
If Foe, our love shall conquer thee.

AUTHOR UNKNOWN

SUCCESS

Success is speaking words of praise,
In cheering other people's ways,
In doing just the best you can,
With every task and every plan,
It's silence when your speech would hurt,
Politeness when your neighbor's curt,
It's deafness when the scandal flows,
And sympathy with others' woes,
It's loyalty when duty calls,
It's courage when disaster falls,

It's patience when the hours are long,
It's found in laughter and in song,
It's in the silent time of prayer,
In happiness and in despair,
In all of life and nothing less,
We find the thing we call success.

AUTHOR UNKNOWN

DON'T GIVE UP

'Twixt failure and success the point's so fine
Men sometimes know not when they touch the line,
Just when the pearl was waiting one more plunge,
How many a struggler has thrown up the sponge!
Then take this honey from the bitterest cup:
"There is no failure save in giving up!"

AUTHOR UNKNOWN

*Of all sad words
of tongue or pen
the saddest are these:*
IT MIGHT HAVE BEEN.

*Let's add this thought
unto this verse:*
IT MIGHT HAVE BEEN
A GREAT DEAL WORSE.

IT MIGHT HAVE BEEN WORSE

Sometimes I pause and sadly think
  Of the things that might have been,
Of the golden chances I let slip by,
  And which never returned again.

Think of the joys that might have been mine;
  The prizes I almost won,
The goals I missed by a mere hair's breadth;
  And the things I might have done.

It fills me with gloom when I ponder thus,
  Till I look on the other side,
How I might have been completely engulfed
  By misfortune's surging tide.

The unknown dangers lurking about,
  Which I passed safely through
The evils and sorrows that I've been spared
  Pass plainly now in review.

So when I am downcast and feeling sad,
  I repeat over and over again,
Things are far from being as bad
  As they easily might have been.

                                G. J. RUSSELL

THE PENDULUM

There was once a pendulum waiting to be fixed on a new clock. It began to calculate how long it would be before the big wheels were worn out and its work was done. It would be expected to tick night and day, so many times a minute, sixty times that every hour, and twenty-four times that every day and three hundred and sixty-five times that every year. It was awful! Quite a row of figures, enough to stagger you! Millions of ticks! "I can never do it," said the poor pendulum. But the clockmaster encouraged it. "You can do one tick at a time?" he said. "Oh, yes," the pendulum could do that. "Well," he said, "that is all that will be required of you." So the pendulum went to work, steadily ticking, one tick at a time, and it is ticking yet, quite cheerfully.

DWIGHT LYMAN MOODY

MISTAKES

God sent us here to make mistakes,
    To strive, to fail, to rebegin,
To taste the tempting fruit of sin,
    And find what bitter food it makes.

To miss the path, to go astray,
    To wander blindly in the night.
But searching, praying for the light,
    Until at last we find the way.

And looking back along the past,
    We know we needed all the strain
Of fear and doubt and strife and pain
    To make us value peace, at last.

Who fails finds later triumph sweet.
    Who stumbles once walks then with care,
And knows the place to cry "Beware"
    To other unaccustomed feet.

Through strife the slumbering soul awakes
    We learn on errors troubled route
The truths we could not prize without
    The sorrow of our sad mistakes.

ELLA WHEELER WILCOX

TO A NEW DAUGHTER-IN-LAW

Forgive me if I speak possessively of him
    Who now is yours, yet still is mine;
Call it the silver cord disparagingly
    And weave new colors in an old design,
Yet know the warp was started long ago
    By faltering steps, by syllable and sound,

By all the years in which I watched him grow. . . .
  By all the seasons' turnings are we bound.
But now, I loose the cord, untie the knot,
  Unravel years so he is yours alone
And if there is a message I forgot
  Or something that could help you had you known,
I shall be waiting, hoping you will see
  That him you love, is also *loved by me.*

AUTHOR UNKNOWN

Take the world as it is!—with its smiles and its sorrow,
  Its love and its friendship—its falsehood and truth—
Its schemes that depend on the breath of tomorrow!
  Its hopes which pass by like the dreams of our youth—
Yet, oh! whilst the light of affection may shine,
  The heart in itself hath a fountain of bliss!
In the *worst* there's some spark of a nature divine,
  And the wisest and best *take the world as it is.*

FROM "TAKE THE WORLD AS IT IS" BY CHARLES SWAIN

A BIRTHDAY WISH

I do not wish you joy without a sorrow,
  Nor endless day without the healing dark,
Nor brilliant sun without the restful shadow,
  Nor tides that never turn against your bark.

I wish you love, and strength, and faith, and wisdom,
Goods, gold enough to help some needy one.
I wish you songs, but also blessed silence,
And God's sweet peace when every day is done.

DOROTHY NELL MCDONALD

O World of green and shafts of golden sun; of nightly, silent silver moonlight; and the strange songs of gentle winds!

O time of dreams, and trysts, and olden memories come to life! Sweet summer, may I sing as thou, for every leaf of thine is pregnant with music in the soft winds. I yield myself to the thousand enchantments of sky and field and wood, and play again like a child on the soft green of the earth.

And as the God of the universe has made thee to bloom in tenderness, so also may my heart be made to bloom again.

MAX EHRMANN

SUNSHINE AND MUSIC

A laugh is just like sunshine.
It freshens all the day,
It tips the peak of life with light,
And drives the clouds away.
The soul grows glad that hears it
And feels its courage strong.
A laugh is just like sunshine
For cheering folks along.

43

A laugh is just like music.
It lingers in the heart,
And where its melody is heard
The ills of life depart;
And happy thoughts come crowding
Its joyful notes to greet:
A laugh is just like music
For making living sweet.

AUTHOR UNKNOWN

Some folks in looks take so much pride
They don't think much of what's inside;
Well, as for me, I know my face
Can ne'er be made a thing of grace
And so I rather think I'll see
How I can fix the inside of me;
So folks'll say, "He looks like sin
But ain't he beautiful within!"

AUTHOR UNKNOWN

THAT'S SUCCESS!

It's doing your job the best you can
And being just to your fellow man;
It's making money—but holding friends
And true to your aims and ends;

It's figuring how and learning why
And looking forward and thinking high
And dreaming a little and doing much.
It's keeping always in closest touch
With what is finest in word and deed;
It's being thorough, yet making speed;
It's daring blithely the field of chance
While making labor a brave romance;
It's going onward despite defeat
And fighting stanchly, but keeping sweet;
It's being clean and it's playing fair;
It's laughing lightly at Dame Despair;
It's looking up at the stars above
And drinking deeply of life and love.
It's struggling on with the will to win
But taking loss with a cheerful grin;
It's sharing sorrow and work and mirth
And making better this good old earth;
It's serving, striving through strain and stress;
It's doing your noblest—that's Success!

BERTON BRALEY

"Two persons cannot long be friends if they cannot for-give each other's little failings."

45

FRIENDSHIP

Oh, the comfort—the inexpressible comfort of feeling safe
    with a person,
Having neither to weigh thoughts,
Nor measure words—but pouring them
All right out—just as they are—
Chaff and grain together—
Certain that a faithful hand will
Take and sift them—
Keep what is worth keeping—
And with the breath of kindness
Blow the rest away.

DINAH MARIA MULOCK CRAIK

"Purchase not friends by gifts; when thou ceasest to give, such will cease to love."

THE DAWN

One morn I rose and looked upon the world.
"Have I been blind until this hour?" I said.
On every trembling leaf the sun had spread,
And was like golden tapestry unfurled;
And as the moments passed more light was hurled

46

Upon the drinking earth athirst for light;
And I, beholding all this wondrous sight,
Cried out aloud, "O God, I love Thy world!"
And since that waking, often I drink deep
The joy of dawn, and peace abides with me;
And though I know that I again shall see
Dark fear with withered hand approach my sleep,
More sure am I when lonely night shall flee,
At dawn the sun will bring good cheer to me.

AUTHOR UNKNOWN

KNOWLEDGE

We search the world for truth,
We cull the good, the pure, the beautiful,
From graven stone and written scroll,
From the old flower-fields of the soul,
And, weary seekers for the best,
We come back laden from our quest,
To find that all the sages said
Is in the Book our mothers read.

AUTHOR UNKNOWN

Our deeds are recorded even to the smallest detail. The recording angel is no myth; it is found in ourselves. It is the law of habit. We spend our lives writing our own biog-

*raphies. Every act, word, and thought leaves an impression
and a tendency that makes repetition easy.*

*We are prone to imitate those about us but most of all we
imitate ourselves. The doing of a thing once makes it easier
to do it again in the same way; and the repetition becomes a
habit, which is almost impossible to break. Habits determine
character, therefore right character building consists of right
habit making.*

How shall I a habit break?
As you did that habit make.
As you gathered, you must lose;
As you yielded, now refuse.
Thread by thread the strands we twist
Till they bind us, neck and wrist.
Thread by thread the patient hand
Must untwine, ere free we stand.
As we builded, stone by stone,
We must toil, unhelped, alone,
Till the wall is overthrown.

FROM "A BUILDER'S LESSON"
BY JOHN BOYLE O'REILLY

Youth fades; love droops; the lessons of friendship fall;
A mother's secret hope outlives them all.

OLIVER WENDELL HOLMES

MOTHER'S HANDS

Dear gentle hands have stroked my hair
  And cooled my brow,
Soft hands that pressed me close
  And seemed to know somehow
Those fleeting moods and erring thoughts
  That cloud my day,
Which quickly melt beneath their suffrage
  And pass away.

No other balm for earthly pain
  Is half so sure,
No sweet caress so filled with love
  Nor half so pure,
No other soul so close akin that understands,
No touch that brings such perfect peace as Mother's hands.

W. DAYTON WEDGEFARTH

Mother in gladness, Mother in sorrow,
Mother today, and Mother tomorrow,
With arms ever open to fold and caress you
O Mother of Mine, may God keep you and bless you.

W. DAYTON WEDGEFARTH

A SMILE

Nothing on earth can smile but man! Gems may flash re-
flected light, but what is a diamond-flash compared to an
eye-flash and a mirth-flash? Flowers cannot smile; this is a
charm that even they cannot claim. It is the prerogative of
man; it is the color which love wears, and cheerfulness, and
joy—these three. It is a light in the windows of the face, by
which the heart signifies it is at home and waiting. A face
that cannot smile is like a bud that cannot blossom, and dries
up on the stalk. Laughter is day, and sobriety is night, and a
smile is the twilight that hovers gently between both—more
bewitching than either.

HENRY WARD BEECHER

Talk not of wasted affection! affection never was wasted;
If it enrich not the heart of another, its waters, returning
Back to their springs, like the rain, shall fill them full of
    refreshment:
That which the fountain sends forth returns again to the
    fountain.

FROM "EVANGELINE" BY HENRY WADSWORTH LONGFELLOW

THE WHOLE DUTY OF A POEM

A poem should be, as our best ever are,
Golden of heart like a rose or a star.

A poem should be, like the brook that you hear
Sing down the mountainside, lovely and clear.

Yet in its music a poem should hold
That which is felt but may never be told.

ARTHUR GUITERMAN

GOD THE ARTIST

God, when you thought of a pine tree,
How did you think of a star?
God, when you patterned a bird song,
Flung on a silver string,
How did you know the ecstasy
That crystal call would bring?
How did you think of a bubbling throat
And a beautifully speckled wing?

God, when you fashioned a raindrop,
How did you think of a stem
Bearing a lovely satin leaf
To hold the tiny gem?
How did you know a million drops
Would deck the morning's hem?

51

Why did you mate the moonlit night
With the honeysuckle vines?
How did you know Madeira bloom
Distilled ecstatic wines?
How did you weave the velvet dusk
Where tangled perfumes are?
God, when you thought of a pine tree,
How did you think of a star?

ANGELA MORGAN

WHO DOES NOT LOVE TRUE POETRY

Who does not love true poetry,
He lacks a bosom friend
  To walk with him
  And talk with him,
And all his steps attend.

Who does not love true poetry—
Its rhythmic throb and swing
  The treat of it
  The sweet of it,
Along the paths of Spring:

Its joyous lilting melody
In every passing breeze,
  The deep of it,
  The sweep of it,
Through hours of toil or ease;

Its grandeur and sublimity—
Its majesty and might—
  The feel of it,
  The peal of it,
Through all the lonely night;

Its tenderness and soothing touch;
Like balm on evening air,
  That feelingly
  And healingly
Cures all the hurts of care:

Who does not love true poetry
Of sea and sky and sod—
  The height of it
  The might of it—
He has not known his God.

HENRY CLAY HALL

Ships that pass in the night, and speak each other in passing,
Only a signal shown and a distant voice in the darkness;
So on the ocean of life we pass and speak one another,
Only a look and a voice; then darkness again and a silence.

FROM "TALES OF A WAYSIDE INN"
BY HENRY WADSWORTH LONGFELLOW

OPEN YOUR EYES

Open your eyes that you may see
The beauty that around you lies,
The misty loveliness of the dawn,
The glowing colors of the skies;
The child's bright eager eyes of blue,
The gnarled and wrinkled face of age,
The bird with crimson on his wing
Whose spirit never knew a cage;
The roadsides' blooming goldenrod
So brave through summer's wind and heat,
The brook that rushes to the sea
With courage that naught may defeat.
Open your eyes that you may see
The wonder that around you lies;
It will enrich your every day
And make you glad and kind and wise.

EMMA BOGE WHISENAND

If all the misfortunes of mankind were cast into a basket, in order to be equally distributed among all, those who now think themselves so unhappy—would much prefer the share they already possess, to that which would fall to them by such a division.

BLIND

"Show me your God!" the doubter cries.
I point him to the smiling skies;
I show him all the woodland greens;
I show him peaceful sylvan scenes;
I show him winter snows and frost;
I show him waters tempest-tossed;
I show him hills rock-ribbed and strong;
I bid him hear the thrush's song;
I show him flowers in the close—
The lily, violet and rose;
I show him rivers, babbling streams;
I show him youthful hopes and dreams;
I show him maids with eager hearts;
I show him toilers in the marts;
I show him stars, the moon, the sun;
I show him deeds of kindness done;
I show him joy; I show him care,
And still he holds his doubting air,
And faithless goes his way, for he
Is blind of soul, and cannot see!

JOHN KENDRICK BANGS

Who builds a church within his heart
And takes it with him everywhere
Is holier far than he whose church
Is but a one-day house of prayer.

MORRIS ABEL BEER

FULFILLMENT

Lo, I have opened unto you the
    gates of my being,
And like a tide, you have flowed
    into me.
The innermost recesses of my spirit
    are full of you
And all the channels of my soul
    are grown sweet with your presence
For you have brought me peace;
    The peace of great tranquil waters,
And the quiet of the summer sea.
    Your hands are filled with peace as
The noon-tide is filled with light;
    About your head is bound the eternal
Quiet of the stars, and in your heart
    dwells the calm miracle of twilight.

I am utterly content.

In all my being is no ripple of unrest
  For I have opened unto you the
Wide gates of my being
  And like a tide, you have flowed into me.

AUTHOR UNKNOWN

HOW OLD ARE YOU?

Age is a quality of mind.
If you have left your dreams behind,
If hope is cold,
If you no longer look ahead,
If your ambitions' fires are dead—
Then you are old.

But if from life you take the best,
And if in life you keep the jest,
If love you hold;
No matter how the years go by,
No matter how the birthdays fly—
You are not old.

H. S. FRITSCH

LITTLE WORDS

"Yes, you did, too!"
"I did not!"
Thus the little quarrel started,
Thus by unkind little words,
Two fond friends were parted.

"I am sorry."
"So am I."
Thus the little quarrel ended,
Thus by loving little words
Two fond hearts were mended.

BENJAMIN KEECH

HELP ME TODAY

This day, I think, will be a common day,
Devoid of venture, risk or thrill or show;
Eight working hours, plodding in a row
Like lagging sheep, whose herder I must be—
And You, who made me, know I hate such days!

I can face danger or the press of haste,
Cruel shock or sudden uproar and alarm,

Or I can laugh and play the merry clown,
Or act a part to mask some desperate need—
But something limps in me when days are dull.

And so I ask Your help this common day.
Help me keep sweet when there is none to see;
Help me be patient though there be no praise,
And brave without the spotlight or applause,
And honest, in the secret, unseen acts.

Dear Friend, whom I can feel but cannot see,
Help me today.

ELSIE ROBINSON

THINKING HAPPINESS

Think of the things that make you happy,
  Not the things that make you sad;
Think of the fine and true in mankind,
  Not its sordid side and bad;
Think of the blessings that surround you,
  Not the ones that are denied;
Think of the virtues of your friendships,
  Not the weak and faulty side;

Think of the gains you've made in business,
  Not the losses you've incurred;
Think of the good of you that's spoken,
  Not some cruel, hostile word;

59

Think of the days of health and pleasure,
  Not the days of woe and pain;
Think of the days alive with sunshine,
  Not the dismal days of rain;

Think of the hopes that lie before you,
  Not the waste that lies behind;
Think of the treasures you have gathered,
  Not the ones you've failed to find;
Think of the service you may render,
  Not of serving self alone;
Think of the happiness of others,
  And in this you'll find your own!

ROBERT E. FARLEY

A GOOD CREED

If any little word of ours
  Can make one life the brighter;
If any little song of ours
  Can make one heart the lighter;
God help us speak that little word,
  And take our bit of singing
And drop it in some lonely vale
  To set the echoes ringing.

If any little love of ours
  Can make one life the sweeter;
If any little care of ours
  Can make one step the fleeter;

If any little help may ease
  The burden of another;
God give us love and care and strength
  To help along each other.

If any little thought of ours
  Can make one life the stronger;
If any cheery smile of ours
  Can make its brightness longer;
Then let us speak that thought today,
  With tender eyes aglowing,
So God may grant some weary one
  Shall reap from our glad sowing.

                    AUTHOR UNKNOWN

Blessed is he who has found his work,
let him ask no other blessedness.

                    CARLYLE

IT'S SIMPLY GREAT

It's great to be alive, and be
  A part of all that's going on;
To live and work and feel and see
  Life lived each day from early dawn;

To rise and with the morning light
   Go forth until the hours grow late,
Then joyously return at night
   And rest from honest toil—it's great!

It's great to be a living part
   Of all the surging world alive,
And lend a hand in field and mart,
   A worker in this human hive;
To live and earn and dare to do,
   Nor ever shirk or deviate
From course or purpose we pursue!
   Until the goal is won—it's great!

It's great to realize that we
   Are of a latent power possessed
To be what we are willed to be,
   And equal unto any test;
That of ourselves we may achieve
   To worthy deeds and high estate,
If we but in our powers believe
   It can and will be done—it's great!

It's great and wonderful to know
   That all we have to do is do,
That if we will to grow we'll grow,
   And reach the mark we have to view;
To know that we're a vital part
   Of all that is, nor hesitate
With all of skill and mind and heart
   To work and win—it's simply great!

SIDNEY WARREN MASE

OUTWITTED

He drew a circle that shut me out—
Heretic, rebel, a thing to flout.
But Love and I had the wit to win:
We drew a circle that took him in!

EDWIN MARKHAM

PRAYER OF AN UNEMPLOYED MAN

Here in the quiet of my room,
I come to Thee for friendship; to feel
That Someone is with me, though unseen.
All day I have seen a multitude of people,
But I am still lonely and hungry for human cheer.

No life has touched mine in understanding;
No hand has clasped mine in friendship;
My heart is empty and my hands are idle.
Help me to feel Thy presence,
So that the disappointment of this day
Shall not overwhelm me.

Keep me from becoming cynical and bitter;
Keep me warm and human, and set a new faith
Before my eyes—a new hope to live by
And a new spirit with which to overcome discouragements.

Guide me to that very necessary thing
Of life—work!
Abide with me and be my friend.

W. C. ACKERLY

THE MONK AND THE PEASANT

A peasant once unthinkingly
  Spread tales about a friend.
But later found the rumors false
  And hoped to make amend.

He sought the counsel of a monk,
  A man esteemed and wise,
Who heard the peasant's story through
  And felt he must advise.

The kind monk said: "If you would have
  A mind again at peace,
I have a plan whereby you may
  From trouble find release.

"Go fill a bag with chicken down
  And to each dooryard go
And lay one fluffy feather where
  The streams of gossip flow."

The peasant did as he was told
  And to the monk returned,
Elated that his penance was
  A thing so quickly earned.

"Not yet," the old monk sternly said,
  "Take up your bag once more
And gather up the feathers that
  You placed at every door."

The peasant, eager to atone,
  Went hastening to obey,
No feathers met his sight, the wind
  Had blown them all away.

MARGARET E. BRUNER

THE SINNER

They whispered when she passed—gave knowing looks
That hinted vastly more than what was said;
Inferring that her past held darkest nooks—
Her reputation was a tattered shred.

And yet, she walked among them calm, serene,
Like one who from deep suffering had found
An inner peace—a staff on which to lean—
It seemed as if she trod on holy ground.

MARGARET E. BRUNER

Sweet are the thoughts that savor of content,
The quiet mind is richer than a crown—
A mind content, both crown and kingdom is.

ROBERT GREENE

AUCTION SALE—HOUSEHOLD FURNISHINGS

"Nothing much here!" they say. With careless glance
And little sly disdainful pokes they pass.
"I only came because there was a chance
Of getting something cheap. But then, this class
Of people seldom has a thing worth while."
Coming and going . . . jibes in every tone.
"There's not much here!" . . . Face frozen in a smile
She stands among them, terribly alone,
Hearing the auctioneer's decisive cries,
Hearing them bid, half mocking, half amused,
Praying, with pain that stabs between the eyes,
That no one wants the mug her baby used,
Clutching her heart when someone takes away
All her young married life in one small dray.

ADELE DE LEEUW

If spring came but once in a century, instead of once a year, or burst forth with the sound of an earthquake, and not in silence, what wonder and expectation there would be in all hearts to behold the miraculous change. But now the silent succession suggests nothing but necessity. To most men only the cessation of the miracle would be miraculous, and the perpetual exercise of God's power seems less wonderful than its withdrawal would be.

HENRY WADSWORTH LONGFELLOW

ALOHA OE

ITS MEANING

It's more than just an easy word for casual good-bye;
It's gayer than a greeting and it's sadder than a sigh;
It has the hurting poignancy, the pathos of a sob;
It's sweeter than a youthful heart's exquisite joyous throb;
It's all the tender messages that words cannot convey;
It's tears unshed, and longing for a loved one gone away;
It's welcome to Hawaii and it's lingering farewell;
It's all the dear and silent things that lovers' lips can tell;
It's woven into flower *leis* and old Hawaiian songs;
It's frailer than a spider-web and strong as leather thongs;
It's fresh as dew on ginger blooms and older than the moon;
It's in the little lullabies that native mothers croon;
It's said a hundred different ways, in sadness and in joy;
Aloha means "I love you." So, I say "Aloha oe."

DON BLANDING

BE KIND

Be kind to thy father: for when thou wert young,
    Who loved thee as fondly as he?
He caught the first accents that fell from thy tongue,
    And joined in thine innocent glee.

Be kind to thy mother: for lo! on her brow
    May traces of sorrow be seen;
Oh, well may'st thou cherish and comfort her now
    For loving and kind hath she been.

Be kind to thy brother: wherever you are,
    The love of a brother shall be
An ornament, purer and richer by far
    Than pearls from the depths of the sea.

Be kind to thy sister: not many may know
    The depth of true sisterly love;
The wealth of the ocean lies fathoms below
    The surface that sparkles above.

Thy kindness shall bring to thee many sweet hours,
    And blessings thy pathway to crown;
Affection shall weave thee a garland of flowers,
    More precious than wealth or renown.

MARGARET COURTNEY

Civilization is just a slow process of learning to be kind.

MEDIATION No. 4891

MEDIATORS

Miss Pearl S. Buck—*Novelist; Nobel Prize Winner*
Dr. Joseph K. Folsom—*Head of Dept. of Sociology, Vassar College*
Rev. Dr. Ralph Emerson Davis

When the sweet language of courtship is over and the mystic words are uttered, "I pronounce you man and wife," the real meaning behind a marriage begins to make itself apparent. With the fear of losing one another removed, true character traits are uncovered, and the other party realizes, often for the first time, strange and new aspects of the nature of his or her marital partner.

The evening that I read the poem, *Any Husband or Wife*, there was a case typical of any number of marriages in which, following the first few months, there is a tendency to take the other for granted. In this instance, the accumulation of small grievances began to loom large and there were charges and countercharges of misplaced trust, selfishness, nagging, disloyalty, etc., etc. Here was a complete shattering of hopes and dreams in a relationship begun in complete good faith.

The poem ends with the significant words: "We shall be lovers when the last door shuts, but what is better still—we shall be friends." Not only in connection with the differences of this particular couple, but as a general thing, there is found in this expression an answer to many a despairing moment in the lives of people who have every reason to live happily with one another but who often permit themselves to engage in the "familiarity that breeds contempt"; who fail to extend to the one nearest and dearest in all the world everyday courtesies ordinarily bestowed upon a friend.

This idea of friendship between husband and wife, based on common courtesy and consideration, is effectively expressed in the words of the poem that follows.

ANY HUSBAND OR WIFE

Let us be guests in one another's house
With deferential "no" and courteous "yes";
Let us take care to hide our foolish moods
Behind a certain show of cheerfulness.

Let us avoid all sullen silences;
We should find fresh and sprightly things to say;
I must be fearful lest you find me dull,
And you must dread to bore me anyway.

Let us knock gently at each other's heart,
Glad of a chance to look within—and yet,
Let us remember that to force one's way
Is the unpardoned breach of etiquette.

So, shall I be host—you, the hostess,
Until all need for entertainment ends;
We shall be lovers when the last door shuts
But what is better still—we shall be friends.

CAROL HAYNES

Man is dear to man: the poorest poor
Long for some moments in a weary life
When they can know and feel that they have been
Themselves the fathers and the givers-out
Of some small blessings; have been kind to such
As needed kindness, for the single cause
That we have all of us one common heart.

WILLIAM WORDSWORTH

LET ME BE A GIVER

God, let me be a giver, and not one
  Who only takes and takes unceasingly;
God, let me give, so that not just my own,
  But others' lives as well, may richer be.

Let me give out whatever I may hold
  Of what material things life may be heaping,
Let me give raiment, shelter, food, or gold
  If these are, through Thy bounty, in my keeping.

But greater than such fleeting treasures, may
I give my faith and hope and cheerfulness,
Belief and dreams and joy and laughter gay
Some lonely soul to bless.

MARY CAROLYN DAVIES

FOUR THINGS

Four things a man must learn to do
If he would make his record true:
To think without confusion clearly;
To love his fellow-men sincerely;
To act from honest motives purely;
To trust in God and heaven securely.

REV. DR. HENRY VAN DYKE

Other things besides these four that a man must learn are how to make a living, to perform his duties well, to control his tongue, to mind his own business, to govern his passions, to keep his head level, to take care of his health, to fix up his accounts, to know the time of day, to economize, to steer clear of mischief, to be mannerly, to pick up knowledge, to keep wide awake, to know a good thing when he sees it, and to avoid all evil, *if he would make his record true.*

I HAVE FOUND SUCH JOY

I have found such joy in simple things;
  A plain, clean room, a nut-brown loaf of bread,
A cup of milk, a kettle as it sings,
  The shelter of a roof above my head,
And in a leaf-laced square along the floor,
Where yellow sunlight glimmers through a door.

I have found such joy in things that fill
  My quiet days: a curtain's blowing grace,
A potted plant upon my window sill,
  A rose, fresh-cut and placed within a vase;
A table cleared, a lamp beside a chair,
And books I long have loved beside me there.

Oh, I have found such joys I wish I might
  Tell every woman who goes seeking far
For some elusive, feverish delight,
  That very close to home the great joys are:
The elemental things—old as the race,
Yet never, through the ages, commonplace.

GRACE NOLL CROWELL

In the school of life many branches of knowledge are
taught. But the only philosophy that amounts to anything
after all, is just the secret of making friends with our luck.

HENRY VAN DYKE

RENDEZVOUS

For just a brief while every day
I steal away from duty
And leave the indoor tasks undone
To keep a tryst with beauty.

Bird-song and lily-bell
Tinkling thin and sweet;
Sun-gold and starry bloom
Flashing at my feet;
Cool mist, with crystal beads
Gleaming everywhere;
Wild plum and pink thorn
Hanging on the air.

Swiftly, then, I can return
To tread the rounds of duty,
Since for one fleet breath I stood
Hand-in-hand with beauty.

MARY SCOTT FITZGERALD

PHILOSOPHY

If there's no Sun, I still can have the Moon;
If there's no Moon, the Stars my needs suffice;
And if these fail, I have my Evening Lamp;
Or, Lampless, there's my trusty Tallow Dip;
And if the Dip goes out, my Couch remains,
Where I may sleep and dream there's Light again.

JOHN KENDRICK BANGS

THE RIGHT KIND OF PEOPLE

Gone is the city, gone the day,
Yet still the story and the meaning stay:
Once where a prophet in the palm shade basked
A traveler chanced at noon to rest his miles.
"What sort of people may they be," he asked,
"In this proud city on the plains o'erspread?"
"Well, friend, what sort of people whence you came?"
"What sort?" the packman scowled; "why, knaves and fools."
"You'll find the people here the same," the wise man said.

Another stranger in the dusk drew near,
And pausing, cried, "What sort of people here
In your bright city where yon towers arise?"
"Well, friend, what sort of people whence you came?"

"What sort?" the pilgrim smiled,
"Good, true and wise."
"You'll find the people here the same,"
The wise man said.

EDWIN MARKHAM

FRIENDSHIP

Friendship needs no studied phrases,
  Polished face, or winning wiles;
Friendship deals no lavish praises,
  Friendship dons no surface smiles.

Friendship follows Nature's diction,
  Shuns the blandishments of Art,
Boldly severs truth from fiction,
  Speaks the language of the heart.

Friendship favors no condition,
  Scorns a narrow-minded creed,
Lovingly fulfills its mission,
  Be it word or be it deed.

Friendship cheers the faint and weary,
  Makes the timid spirit brave,
Warns the erring, lights the dreary,
  Smooths the passage to the grave.

Friendship—pure, unselfish friendship,
All through life's allotted span,
Nurtures, strengthens, widens, lengthens,
Man's relationship with man.

AUTHOR UNKNOWN

TO HUSBAND AND WIFE

Preserve sacredly the privacies of your own house, your married state and your heart. Let no one ever presume to come between you or share the joys or sorrows that belong to you two alone.

With mutual help, build your quiet world, not allowing your dearest earthly friend to be the confidant of aught that concerns your domestic peace. Let moments of alienation, if they occur, be healed at once. Never, never, speak of it outside; but to each other confess, and all will come out right. Never let the morrow's sun still find you at variance. Renew and renew your vow. It will do you good; and thereby your minds will grow together contented in that love which is stronger than death, and you will be truly one.

AUTHOR UNKNOWN

God grant me the serenity
To accept the things I cannot change;
The courage to change the things I can;
And the wisdom to know the difference.

REINHOLD NIEBUHR

IF YOU MADE GENTLER THE
CHURLISH WORLD

If you have spoken something beautiful,
Or touched the dead canvas to life,
Or made the cold stone to speak—
You who know the secret heart of beauty;
If you have done one thing
That has made gentler the churlish world,
Though mankind pass you by,
And feed and clothe you grudgingly—
Though the world starve you,
And God answer not your nightly prayers,
And you grow old hungering still at heart,
And walk friendless in your way,
And lie down at last forgotten—
If all this befall you who have created beauty,
You shall still leave a bequest to the world
Greater than institutions and riches and commerce;
And by the immutable law of the human heart
The God of the universe is your debtor,
If you have made gentler the churlish world.

MAX EHRMANN

FORGIVEN

You left me when the weary weight of sorrow
  Lay, like a stone, upon my bursting heart;
It seemed as if no shimmering tomorrow
  Could dry the tears that you had caused to start.
You left me, never telling why you wandered—
  Without a word, without a last caress;
Left me with but the love that I had squandered,
  The husks of love and a vast loneliness.

And yet if you came back with arms stretched toward me,
  Came back tonight, with carefree, smiling eyes,
And said: "My journeying has somehow bored me,
  And love, though broken, never, never dies!"
I would forget the wounded heart you gave me,
  I would forget the bruises on my soul.
My old-time gods would rise again to save me;
  My dreams would grow supremely new and whole.
What though youth lay, a tattered garment, o'er you?
  Warm words would leap upon my lips, long dumb;
If you came back, with arms stretched out before you,
  And told me, dear, that you were glad to come!

MARGARET E. SANGSTER

MY WAGE

I bargained with Life for a penny,
   And Life would pay no more,
However I begged at evening
   When I counted my scanty store;

For Life is a just employer,
   He gives you what you ask,
But once you have set the wages,
   Why, you must bear the task.

I worked for a menial's hire,
   Only to learn, dismayed,
That any wage I had asked of Life,
   Life would have paid.

JESSIE B. RITTENHOUSE

WHILE WE MAY

I am going your way, so let us go hand in hand. You help
me and I'll help you. We shall not be here forever. One day
the kind old nurse will come and rock us all to sleep. Let
us help one another while we may.

AUTHOR UNKNOWN

GOOD-BY

We say it for an hour, or for years;
We say it smiling, say it choked with tears;
We say it coldly, say it with a kiss;
And yet we have no other word than this—
            "Good-by."

We have no dearer word for our heart's friend,
For him who journeys to the world's far end,
And scars our soul with going; thus we say,
As unto him who steps but o'er the way—
            "Good-by."

Alike to those we love and those we hate,
We say no more in parting. At life's gate,
To him who passes out beyond earth's sight,
We cry, as to the wanderer for a night—
            "Good-by."

GRACE DENIO LITCHFIELD

THE HOUSE OF PRIDE

I lived with Pride; the house was hung
  With tapestries of rich design.
Of many houses, this among
  Them all was richest, and 'twas mine.
But in the chambers burned no fire,
  Tho' all the furniture was gold:
I sickened of fulfilled desire,
  The House of Pride was very cold.

I lived with Knowledge; very high
  Her house rose on a mountain's side.
I watched the stars roll through the sky,
  I read the scroll of Time flung wide.
But in that house, austere and bare,
  No children played, no laughter clear
Was heard, no voice of mirth was there,
  The House was high but very drear.

I lived with Love; all she possest
  Was but a tent beside a stream.
She warmed my cold hands in her breast,
  She wove around my sleep a dream.
And One there was with face divine
  Who softly came, when day was spent,
And turned our water into wine,
  And made our life a sacrament.

WILLIAM J. DAWSON

OL' CLOTHES

The Junk Man passed the house today
And gave his call in his plaintive way,
   "Ol' clothes!
     Ol' clothes!
      Ol' Clothes!
  Any ol' clothes to throw away?
  Any ol' dishes . . . any ol' plates,
  Any ol' pants or hats or skates,
  Any ol' kettles or pots or pans,
  Any ol' bottles or ol' tin cans,
  Any ol' dresses or any ol' shoes,
  Any ol' things that you can't use?
   Ol' clothes!
    Ol' clothes!
     Ol' clothes!"

I searched the house and made a heap
Of things that I didn't need to keep,
Outworn garments and out-read books,
Clothes that had hung on rusty hooks
For the dust to grime and the moths to chew.
And thus the old made way for the new.
I thought, as the old man went his way,
How grand it would be if every day
The Junk Man passed the house to say,
  "Ol' woes
   Ol' woes
    Ol' woes

Any ol' woes to throw away?
Any ol' grudges . . . any ol' hates,
Any ol' miseries or sad ol' dates,
Any ol' sorrows or any ol' spites,
Any ol' fusses or feuds or fights,
Any ol' sighs or any ol' tears,
Any ol' wishing for yesteryears,
Any ol' quarrels or any ol' frets,
Any ol' tears or ol' regrets?
  Ol' woes!
    Ol' woes!
      Ol' woes!"

AUTHOR UNKNOWN

MORNING PRAYER

When little things would irk me, and I grow
Impatient with my dear ones, make me know
How in a moment joy can take its flight
And happiness be quenched in endless night.
Keep this thought with me all the livelong day
That I may guard the harsh words I might say
When I would fret and grumble, fiery hot,
At trifles that tomorrow are forgot—
Let me remember, Lord, how it would be
If these, my loved ones, were not here with me.

AUTHOR UNKNOWN

There's no defeat in life
Save from within,
Unless you're beaten there
You're bound to win.

EQUIPMENT

Figure it out for yourself, my lad,
You've all that the greatest of men have had,
Two arms, two hands, two legs, two eyes
And brain to use if you would be wise.
With this equipment they all began,
So start for the top and say, "I can."

Look them over, the wise and great,
They take their food from a common plate,
And similar knives and forks they use,
With similar laces they tie their shoes,
The world considers them brave and smart,
But you've all they had when they made their start.

You can triumph and come to skill,
You can be great if you only will.
You're well equipped for what fight you choose,
You have legs and arms and a brain to use,
And the man who has risen great deeds to do
Began his life with no more than you.

You are the handicap you must face,
You are the one who must choose your place,
You must say where you want to go,
How much you will study the truth to know.
God has equipped you for life, but He
Lets you decide what you want to be.

Courage must come from the soul within,
The man must furnish the will to win.
So figure it out for yourself, my lad.
You were born with all that the great have had,
With your equipment they all began
Get hold of yourself, and say: *"I can."*

EDGAR A. GUEST

The year's at the spring
And day's at the morn;
Morning's at seven;
The hillside's dew-pearled;
The lark's on the wing;
The snail's on the thorn;
God's in his heaven—
All's right with the world.

FROM "PIPPA PASSES"
ROBERT BROWNING

PRAYER FOR THIS HOUSE

May nothing evil cross this door,
And may ill fortune never pry
About these windows; may the roar
    And rain go by.

Strengthened by faith, these rafters will
Withstand the batt'ring of the storm;
This hearth, though all the world grow chill,
    Will keep us warm.

Peace shall walk softly through these rooms,
Touching our lips with holy wine,
Till ev'ry casual corner blooms
    Into a shrine.

Laughter shall drown the raucous shout;
And, though these shelt'ring walls are thin,
May they be strong to keep hate out
    And hold love in.

               LOUIS UNTERMEYER

NO FRIEND LIKE MUSIC

There is no whispering of any friend,
  No solace that can touch the quivering heart
In that lone hour when a sudden end
  Has captured laughter and there falls apart
A rainbow that has bridged a distant hill;
  When roses shatter on the stem, and dark
Crowds out the candle's shimmering flame and still
  The night creeps on with neither torch nor spark.

No friend like music when the last word's spoken
  And every pleading is a plea in vain;
No friend like music when the heart is broken,
  To mend its wings and give it flight again;
No friend like music, breaking chains and bars
To let the soul march with the quiet stars!

DANIEL WHITEHEAD HICKY

THANK YOU, GOD

Life can hold such lovely things!
Apple-blossom-scented springs;
Purple mist of haze and heather;
Books to read in stormy weather.

Common as a cooky jar,
Things I hold the dearest are:
A small white house, a small brown dog;
Sunlight breaking through a fog;
And as sweet as summer rain,
Understanding after pain.
Life holds all these lovely things.
Thank you, God, for all it brings.

NINA STILES

MY CREED

This is my creed: To do some good,
    To bear my ills without complaining,
To press on as a brave man should
    For honors that are worth the gaining;
To seek no profits where I may,
    By winning them, bring grief to others;
To do some service day by day
    In helping on my toiling brothers.

This is my creed: To close my eyes
    To little faults of those around me;
To strive to be when each day dies
    Some better than the morning found me;
To ask for no unearned applause,
    To cross no river until I reach it;
To see the merit of the cause
    Before I follow those who preach it. . . .

To keep my standards always high,
    To find my task and always do it:
This is my creed—I wish that I
    Could learn to shape my action to it.

S. E. KISER

BEAUTY AS A SHIELD

I will hold beauty as a shield against despair.
When my heart faints I will remember sights like these:
Bronze cypresses that framed a sapphire sea,
A desert mesa wrapped in sunset flame,
An airplane that raced the Overland
Above a trail still marked with whitening bones;
A path through a dim forest, hushed and sweet,
Lit by one amber beam that fell aslant;
Foam, silver-laced, along a curving wave;
Sprawled golden hills, with shadows like spilled wine;
Tall office buildings rearing through the night
Sheer walls of alabaster pierced with gold—
And snowflakes falling on a lonely pine.

I will hold beauty as a shield against despair.
When my heart faints I will remember sights like these:
The dawning wonder in a baby's face,
The kindness in a weary wanton's smile,
The gallant challenge of a cripple's grin,
Seeing forever bodies that are straight;
The fighting courage in a mother's eyes

When she waits, braced, to meet birth's gripping pains;
The shy adoring of a boy's first love,
The eager beauty of his first crusade
Against some wrong which he alone can right—
The tolerance that sometimes comes with age.

When my heart faints I will remember sights like these,
Holding their beauty as a shield against despair:
For if I can see glory such as this
With my dim eyes, my undeveloped brain,
And if from other darkened, selfish lives
Such flashes of brave loveliness can come,
Then surely there is something more than this
Sad maze of pain, bewilderment and fear—
And if there's something, I can still hope on.

ELSIE ROBINSON

TOGETHER

You and I by this lamp with these
Few books shut out the world. Our knees
Touch almost in this little space.
But I am glad. I see your face.
The silences are long, but each
Hears the other without speech.
And in this simple scene there is
The essence of all subtleties,
The freedom from all fret and smart,
The one sure sabbath of the heart.

The world—we cannot conquer it,
Nor change the minds of fools one whit.
Here, here alone do we create
Beauty and peace inviolate;
Here night by night and hour by hour
We build a high impregnable tower
Whence may shine, now and again,
A light to light the feet of men
When they see the rays thereof:
And this is marriage, this is love.

LUDWIG LEWISOHN

TOYS

My little son, who look'd from thoughtful eyes
And mov'd and spoke in quiet grown-up wise,
Having my law the seventh time disobey'd,
I struck him, and dismiss'd
With hard words and unkiss'd,—
His mother, who was patient, being dead.
Then, fearing lest his grief should hinder sleep,
I visited his bed, but found him slumbering deep
With darken'd eyelids, and their lashes yet
From his late sobbing wet.
And I with moan,
Kissing away his tears, left others of my own;
For, on a table drawn beside his head,
He had put within his reach,
A box of counters and a red-vein'd stone,
A piece of glass abrased by the beach,

And six or seven shells,
A bottle with bluebells
And two French copper coins,—ranged there with careful
    art,
To comfort his sad heart.
So, when that night I pray'd
To God, I wept and said;
"Ah, when at last we lie with muted breath,
Not vexing Thee in death,
And Thou rememberest of what toys
We make our joys,
How weakly understood
Thy great commanded good,—
Then, fatherly not less
Than I whom Thou hast moulded from the clay,
Thou'lt leave Thy wrath, and say,
I will be sorry for their childishness."

COVENTRY PATMORE

A PRAYER

Let me do my work each day;
And if the darkened hours of anxiety overcome me,
May I not forget the strength that comforted me
In the desolation of other times.
May I still remember the bright hours that found me
Walking over the silent hills of earlier days,
Or dreaming on the margin of the quiet river . . .

When I vowed to have courage
Amid the tempests of the changing years.
Spare me from bitterness
And from the sharp passions of unguarded moments.
May I not forget that poverty and true riches are of the
    spirit.
Though the world know me not,
May my thoughts and actions be such
As shall keep me friendly with myself . . .
Give me a few friends who will love me for what I am;
And keep ever burning before my vagrant steps
The kindly light of hope.
And though age and infirmity overtake me,
And I come not within sight of the castle of my dreams,
Teach me still to be thankful for life,
And for time's olden memories that are good and sweet;
And may the evening's twilight find me gentle still.

MAX EHRMANN

SHABBY OLD DAD

His collar is frayed, and his trousers unpressed;
He's not a bit fussy the way he is dressed,
But he's always ready to help out the rest—
   Shabby old Dad!

His shirts have queer stripes, and they're old-fashioned
    quite;
His ties are in strings, and they're never tied right.
His last year's straw hat is a terrible sight—
    Shabby old Dad!

His shoes need a shine, and his cuff links are tin;
He does sometimes shave, but his top hair is thin;
You hardly would say he was neat as a pin—
    Shabby old Dad!

Shabby old Dad, with his heart full of woes,
And so much to think of besides buying clothes;
With the kids needing food, and the money! God knows!—
    Shabby old Dad!

If there is a Heaven where peace can enfold
A life lived for others, a heart that's pure gold,
He'll go there and live there in glory untold—
    Shabby old Dad!

ANNE CAMPBELL

A BARGAIN SALE

I'm offering for sale today
    A lot of things I'll need no more;
Come, please, and take them all away,
    I've piled them up outside my door.

I'll make the prices low enough,
    And trust you, if it's trust you need;
Here I have listed all my stuff,
    Make your selection as you read:

A lot of prejudices which
    Have ceased to be of use to me;
A stock of envy of the rich,
    Some slightly shopworn jealousy;
A large supply of gloom that I
    Must not permit to clog my shelves;
I offer bargains—who will buy?
    Name prices that will suit yourselves.

A lot of wishes I've outgrown,
    A stock of silly old beliefs;
Some pride I once was proud to own,
    A bulky line of dreads and griefs;
An old assortment of ill will,
    A job lot of bad faith and doubt,
Harsh words that have their poison still;
    Choose as you please—I'm closing out.

I need more room for kindliness,
    For hope and courage and good cheer,
Take all the hatred I possess,
    The superstitions and the fear;
A large supply of frailties I
    Shall have no use for from today;
I offer bargains; who will buy?
    The rubbish must be cleared away!

                              S. E. KISER

God never made a fish with fins until He made an ocean for it to swim in. God never made a bird until He made an atmosphere for it to fly in. And God never put the longings for immortality in a soul until He made a Heaven to satisfy these longings.

AUTHOR UNKNOWN

MEDIATION No. 11087

MEDIATORS

Mr. Ben Hecht—*Author and Playwright*
Hon. Ellsworth B. Buck—*President, Board of Education, City of New York*
Rev. Dr. L. Wendell Fifield

The story of the ingratitude of children after a lifetime of trial and sacrifice on the part of parents is as familiar as it is difficult to understand. Here is a typical case. Several years ago an old woman of seventy, widowed for many years and mother of four children, was prepared to enter a home for the aged. She had been left a fairly substantial sum by her husband but in the twenty years since his death had given a considerable amount to her grown children to help establish them in life. There were still $3000 available, more than sufficient to guarantee care in a home for the rest of her days, insure decent burial, etc.

Previous to this time the question of where this old lady was to live had been the subject of bitter feeling among her several children (all married and with families), principally because of jealousy among them over real or fancied benefits received by others and denied them. Aside from this, the old mother's sight was becoming affected, and she was anxious to settle down and live her remaining years in peace. As arrangements were being completed for her entrance into the home, her eldest son, a man of forty-eight, came to her and pleaded, "Mother, why don't you spend the rest of your life with me? I have been hit hard by conditions. Unless I raise some money at once I shall be wiped out. You can come and live with us comfortably and happily for the rest of your years." Against her better judgment, but unable to refuse this plea for help from her first-born, she accepted this "offer" and handed over to him her last penny, trusting in his promise that he would not fail her.

The rest may be readily imagined. The other children, already resentful toward this brother, who had always been more affluent than they, vexed because of the mother's action, ceased speaking to both mother and brother. The latter, unable to recover his losses, went deeper and deeper into debt. In the meantime his wife, a shrewish type, had made life utterly miserable for the "old woman," segregating her at meals, forbidding the children to converse with her, etc. The son, while conscious of the wrong he had done, was, nevertheless, under the complete domination of his vixenish wife, and exactly ten months after taking her in he ashamedly informed his mother that since he could no longer sustain his home and since hard feeling existed it would be best for her to make arrangements to leave. "When I get on my feet again I will be sure to take care of you," was his only reassurance.

The alternative for the broken and disillusioned old woman was to apply for the old-age pension. Her application was refused because of the existence of the children. It was at this point that the case came to the attention of the board. All of the children were summoned to the mediation proceeding and as can well be imagined shifted responsibility for this poor soul one to the other, with an assortment of reasons that was truly amazing. The principal excuse, of course, was their indignation over her ill-fated decision to cast her lot with the eldest brother. After much show of spite and recrimination the matter was settled, with the four (including the once-affluent brother) signing to contribute several dollars a week each toward her maintenance. At last accounts the sweet old lady was living in comparative peace with a distant cousin, much perplexed, reflecting on life's strange ways, but still the first to show concern when any of the children were "in trouble." The poem which seemed most appropriate for the highly interesting occasion that featured this episode was titled *The Old Mother*.

THE OLD MOTHER

Poor old lady, set her aside—
   Her children are grown, and her work is done;
True, in their service, her locks turned gray,
   But shove her away, unsought, alone.

Give her a home, for decency's sake,
   In some back room, far out of the way,
Where her tremulous voice cannot be heard—
   It might check your mirth when you would be gay.

Strive to forget how she toiled for you
   And cradled you oft on her loving breast—
Told you stories and joined your play,
   Many an hour when she needed rest.

No matter for that—huddle her off;
   Your friends might wince at her witty jest;
She is too old-fashioned, and speaks so plain—
   Get her out of the way of the coming guest.

Once you valued her cheerful voice,
   Her hearty laugh and her merry song;
But to ears polite they are quite too loud—
   Her jokes too sharp, her tales too long.

So, poor old lady, hustle her off—
   In her cheerless room let her sit alone;
She must not meet with your guests tonight,
   For her children are grown and her work is done.

AUTHOR UNKNOWN

THE RIDDLE

Where's an old woman to go when the years
Leave her alone with her sighs and her tears,
Gray-haired and penniless, feeble and slow—
Where's an old woman to go?

What's an old woman to do when her kin
Fail to remember that hands, worn and thin,
Cared for them, slaved for them, all the years through—
What's an old woman to do?

What's an old woman's reward for a life
Given to others as Mother and Wife,
Leaving her faltering, furrowed and scored—
What's an old woman's reward?

                                        H. E. H.

THE LESSON OF THE WATER MILL

Listen to the water mill:
    Through the livelong day
How the clanking of the wheel
    Wears the hours away;

. . . .

And a proverb haunts my mind
  As a spell is cast:
"The mill will never grind
  With the water that has passed."
Take the lesson to thyself,
  Loving heart and true;
Golden years are fleeting by,
  Youth is passing, too;
Learn to make the most of life;
  Lose no happy day;
Time will never bring thee back
  Chances swept away.
Leave no tender word unsaid;
  Love while life shall last;
"The mill will never grind
  With the water that has passed."

. . . .

Take the proverb to thine heart,
  Take! Oh, hold it fast:
"The mill will never grind
  With the water that has passed!"

SARAH DOUDNEY

WEIGHING THE BABY

How many pounds does the baby weigh—
  Baby who came but a month ago?
How many pounds from the crowning curl
  To the rosy point of the restless toe?

Grandfather ties the 'kerchief knot,
  Tenderly guides the swinging weight,
And carefully over his glasses peers
  To read the record "only eight."

Softly the echo goes around:
  The father laughs at the tiny girl;
The fair young mother sings the words,
  While grandmother smooths the golden curl.

And stooping above the precious thing,
  Nestles a kiss, within a prayer.
Murmuring softly, "Little one,
  Grandfather didn't weigh you fair."

Nobody weighed the baby's smile,
  Or the love that came with the helpless one;
Nobody weighed the threads of care,
  From which a woman's life is spun . . .

Nobody weighed the baby's soul
  For here on earth, no weights there be
That would avail. God only knows
  Its value in eternity . . .

                              ETHEL LYNN BEERS

OLD MOTHERS

I love old mothers—mothers with white hair
And kindly eyes, and lips grown softly sweet,
With murmured blessings over sleeping babes.
There is a something in their quiet grace
That speaks the calm of Sabbath afternoons;
A knowledge in their deep, unfaltering eyes
That far outreaches all philosophy.

Time, with caressing touch about them weaves
The silver-threaded fairy-shawl of age,
While all the echoes of forgotten songs
Seem joined to lend a sweetness to their speech.

Old mothers!—as they pass with slow-timed step,
Their trembling hands cling gently to youth's strength.
Sweet mothers!—as they pass, one sees again
Old garden walks, old roses, and old loves.

CHARLES SARSFIELD ROSS

COURTESY

Courtesy is a quality of soul refinement impossible to purchase, impossible to acquire at easy cost.

Politeness is but the shallow imitation of courtesy, and often masquerades as a refining quality in life when it is courtesy that truly refines mankind. Politeness can be assumed, courtesy never. One can be trained upon the surface of the mind, the other must be born in the soul.

Noble natures are often impolite, often lack surface politeness, but have real courtesy in the soul, where great and good men really live. They would not, they could not stoop to low cunning or contemptible meanness.

Polite people may be the very quintessence of cunning, so artful that the world regards them as delightful people until their shallow souls are uncovered. The difference between the polite person and the courteous soul is as wide as the gulf that separates evil from good.

F. E. ELWELL

TO MY SON

Do you know that your soul is of my soul such part,
That you seem to be fibre and cord of my heart?
None other can pain me as you, dear, can do,
None other can please me or praise me as you.

Remember the world will be quick with its blame
If shadow or stain ever darken your name,
"Like mother like son" is a saying so true,
The world will judge largely of "Mother" by you.

Be yours then the task, if task it shall be
To force the proud world to do homage to me,
Be sure it will say when its verdict you've won,
"She reaped as she sowed, Lo! this is her son."

MARGARET JOHNSTON GRIFFIN

A BRIDGE INSTEAD OF A WALL

They say a wife and husband, bit by bit,
Can rear between their lives a mighty wall,
So thick they can not talk with ease through it,
Nor can they see across, it stands so tall!
Its nearness frightens them but each alone
Is powerless to tear its bulk away,
And each, dejected, wishes he had known
For such a wall, some magic thing to say.

So let us build with master art, my dear,
A bridge of faith between your life and mine,
A bridge of tenderness and very near
A bridge of understanding, strong and fine—
Till we have formed so many lovely ties
There never will be room for walls to rise!

AUTHOR UNKNOWN

FOR SALE OR RENT

Upon the house a crooked sign
Succinctly said, "For Sale or Rent";
The bugles on the trumpet-vine
Proclaimed their shocked astonishment,
While all the morning-glory eyes
Were closed against their hurt surprise.

The threshold which no alien feet
Had pressed, became a thoroughfare
For commoners from off the street,
Who came to pry around and stare
At gentlefolk, whose one regard
Seemed fear of trampling up the yard.

But in behind the shuttered pane,
Two old ones sat with folded hands
And lips compressed, not to complain
Although they lost their farms and lands
And all their slender livelihood.
They had each other—God was Good!

AUTHOR UNKNOWN

I SAW TWO CLOUDS AT MORNING

I saw two clouds at morning,
  Tinged with the rising sun,
And in the dawn they floated on,
  And mingled into one:
I thought that morning cloud was blest,
It moved so sweetly to the west.

I saw two summer currents
  Flow smoothly to their meeting,
And join their course, with silent force,
  In peace each other greeting:
Calm was their course through banks of green,
While dimpling eddies played between.

Such be your gentle motion,
  Till life's last pulse shall beat;
Like summer's beam, and summer's stream,
  Float on, in joy, to meet
A calmer sea, where storms shall cease—
A purer sky, where all is peace.

                    JOHN GARDINER BRAINARD

YOU NEVER CAN TELL

You never can tell when you send a word
  Like an arrow shot from a bow
By an archer blind, be it cruel or kind,
  Just where it may chance to go.
It may pierce the breast of your dearest friend,
  Tipped with its poison or balm,
To a stranger's heart in life's great mart
  It may carry its pain or its calm.

You never can tell when you do an act
  Just what the result will be,
But with every deed you are sowing a seed,
  Though the harvest you may not see.
Each kindly act is an acorn dropped
  In God's productive soil;
You may not know, but the tree shall grow
  With shelter for those who toil.

You never can tell what your thoughts will do
  In bringing you hate or love,
For thoughts are things, and their airy wings
  Are swifter than carrier doves.
They follow the law of the universe—
  Each thing must create its kind,
And they speed o'er the track to bring you back
  Whatever went out from your mind.

ELLA WHEELER WILCOX

FOR ONE LATELY BEREFT

Though now you are bereft and ways seem black,
  With emptiness and gloom on every hand;
Someday Time's healing touch will lead you back,
  And gradually your heart will understand
That what you bore must come to one and all,
  And Peace, the clean white flower born of pain,
Will slowly, surely, rise from sorrow's pall,
  And happiness will come to you again.

MARGARET E. BRUNER

I PONDER ON LIFE

I ponder on life:
On fame and unrequited toil,
On anxious young men and young women
Troubled in the day of their dreams,
On hard-pressed men of trade,
And the public cheat held in high esteem;
On the patient artist buying with his youth
That which he shall gain in age
But cannot enjoy, the day of pleasure being past;
On the young man striving to think of God;
I ponder on the tragedy of idealists
Living in a very real world,
On ministers grown larger than their doctrine,
On the chance-taker who has lost,
And on him who has won;
On proud, idle women,
And humble toiling ones;
On the tired worker in the shop,
And the troubled master in the shop,
And jobless men wandering, ever wandering;
On solitary women who sit in gloom,
On the bride and the bridegroom
And the secret chamber that is theirs,
On the dead love of them that still live,
On the mystery of the mother's love,
And the agony of ungrateful children loved;
On lonely sailors out at sea,
Ever watching for hidden death;

On mad dictators of trembling nations,
And the agonies of wars;
I ponder on myself, indifferently honest,
Breathless on the roaring highway of time.
Let me forgive much, forget more,
Remembering only what is beautiful,
That in my day dreams
The picture may grow softer and stiller,
And life again grow gentle.

MAX EHRMANN

THE CLOWN

A crowd was gathering beneath the tent—
    The clown must keep them in a happy mood;
    No matter if the jokes are rough and rude,
A circus is a place for merriment.
And one must be quick-minded and invent
    New tricks and let no saddened thoughts intrude,
    Nor let the public see him sigh or brood,
But banish care and seem indifferent.

There came a lull—I saw him lean awhile
    Against a post and gaze with weary eyes,
As if he traveled backward many a mile. . . .
    And though his body wore a gay disguise,
For one brief space he played a tragic role—
There is no mask to hide a lonely soul.

MARGARET E. BRUNER

SHALL I COMPLAIN?

Shall I complain because the feast is o'er,
 And all the banquet lights have ceased to shine?
 For Joy that was, and is no longer mine;
For Love that came and went, and comes no more;
For Hopes and Dreams that left my open door;
 Shall I, who hold the Past in fee, repine?
 Nay! there are those who never quaffed Life's wine—
That were the unblest fate one might deplore.
To sit alone and dream, at set of sun,
 When all the world is vague with coming night—
 To hear old voices whisper, sweet and low,
And see dear faces steal back, one by one,
 And thrill anew to each long-past delight—
 Shall I complain, who still this Bliss may know?

LOUISE CHANDLER MOULTON

THE FRIEND WHO JUST
STANDS BY

When trouble comes your soul to try,
You love the friend who just "stands by."
Perhaps there's nothing he can do—
The thing is strictly up to you;
For there are troubles all your own,
And paths the soul must tread alone;

Times when love cannot smooth the road
Nor friendship lift the heavy load,
But just to know you have a friend
Who will "stand by" until the end,
Whose sympathy through all endures,
Whose warm handclasp is always yours—
It helps, someway, to pull you through,
Although there's nothing he can do.
And so with fervent heart you cry,
"God bless the friend who just 'stands by'!"

B. Y. WILLIAMS

MEDIATION No. 10871

MEDIATORS

Mr. Channing Pollock—*Author and Playwright*
Mr. Arthur Garfield Hays—*Attorney*
Dr. Theodore F. Savage—*President, Greater
New York Federation of Churches*

This is an issue between a worried mother and her strikingly beautiful daughter. It concerns the strange absence of friends in the latter's life. The mother claimed that she had sacrificed since this twenty-year-old daughter was a child in order to give her everything possible in the way of educational and cultural advantages. She said the only reward ever hoped for was the satisfaction of seeing the girl achieve happiness and contentment. The troubled mother bewailed the fact that this daughter sat home evenings, brooding and lonely, obviously unable to establish the outside contacts and interests so necessary to a full life. The girl reluctantly admitted she did not have one person of either sex she could really call her friend. This was entirely beyond the mother's understanding, especially in view of the girl's rather unusual attractiveness and accomplishments. The differences between mother and daughter as to the reasons for this situation had created considerable irritation and unpleasantness.

The girl appeared with her mother to settle the issue of how it was possible for a young woman of her attainments to be lonely in the city of New York, notwithstanding its numberless opportunities for social, cultural and human contacts. She was employed in an exclusive New York specialty shop but had not chosen to join the employees' organization. She insisted that it was virtually impossible for one with her interests to find the right kind of friends, especially the type she wanted. Since she could not meet the kind of people she felt were especially desirable and since she apparently was not sought out, she remained at home, wondering why she did not have any friends.

It was perfectly plain that this girl, quite without realizing it, had many of the attributes of a snob, that she might easily have attracted desirable friends if she were not so completely wrapped up in herself as to fail to show interest of any kind in other people or enlist her talents and energies in some good cause. She was likened to Narcissus, the mythological character who fell in love with his own reflection which he saw in the water. She had given no thought to Emerson's statement that "to have a friend, one must be a friend."

SEEDS OF KINDNESS

If you have a friend worth loving,
  Love him. Yes, and let him know
That you love him, ere life's evening
  Tinge his brow with sunset glow.
Why should good words ne'er be said
Of a friend—till he is dead?

If you hear a song that thrills you,
  Sung by any child of song,
Praise it. Do not let the singer
  Wait deserved praises long.
Why should one who thrills your heart
Lack the joy you may impart?

If you hear a prayer that moves you
  By its humble, pleading tone,
Join it. Do not let the seeker
  Bow before his God alone.
Why should not your brother share
The strength of "two or three" in prayer?

If you see the hot tears falling
  From a brother's weeping eyes
Share them. And by kindly sharing
  Own your kinship in the skies.
Why should anyone be glad
When another's heart is sad?

If a silvery laugh goes rippling
   Through the sunshine on his face,
Share it. 'Tis the wise man's saying—
   For both grief and joy a place.
There's health and goodness in the mirth
In which an honest laugh has birth.

If your work is made more easy
   By a friendly, helping hand,
Say so. Speak out brave and truly
   Ere the darkness veil the land.
Should a fellow worker near
Falter for a word of cheer?

Scatter thus your seeds of kindness
   All enriching as you go—
Leave them. Trust the Harvest-giver;
   He will make each seed to grow.
So until the happy end,
Your life shall never lack a friend.

AUTHOR UNKNOWN

That best portion of a good man's life—
   His little, nameless, unremembered acts
   Of kindness and of love.

WILLIAM WORDSWORTH

A WOMAN'S QUESTION

Do you know you have asked for the costliest thing
    Ever made by the Hand above?
A woman's heart, and a woman's life—
    And a woman's wonderful love.

Do you know you have asked for this priceless thing
    As a child might ask for a toy?
Demanding what others have died to win,
    With the reckless dash of a boy.

You have written my lesson of duty out;
    Manlike, you have questioned me.
Now stand at the bar of my woman's soul
    Until I shall question thee.

You require your mutton shall be always hot,
    Your socks and your shirt be whole;
I require your heart to be true as God's stars
    And as pure as His heaven your soul.

You require a cook for your mutton and beef;
    I require a far greater thing;
A seamstress you're wanting for socks and shirts—
    I look for a man and a king.

A king for the beautiful realm called Home,
And a man that his Maker, God,
Shall look upon as He did on the first
And say: "It is very good."

I am fair and young, but the rose may fade
From my soft young cheek one day;
Will you love me then 'mid the falling leaves,
As you did 'mong the blossoms of May?

Is your heart an ocean so strong and deep,
I may launch my all on its tide?
A loving woman finds heaven or hell
On the day she is made a bride.

I require all things that are grand and true,
All things that a man should be;
If you give this all, I would stake my life
To be all you demand of me.

If you cannot be this, a laundress and cook
You can hire and little to pay;
But a woman's heart and a woman's life
Are not to be won that way.

LENA LATHROP

The best thing to give to your enemy is forgiveness; to an opponent, tolerance; to a friend, your heart; to your child, a good example; to a father, deference; to your mother, conduct that will make her proud of you; to yourself, respect; to all men, charity.

LORD BALFOUR

BLIND

I cannot view the bloom upon the rose,
    But oh, the scent is very dear to me;
And I can feel the cooling breeze that blows
    Thro' pearl-tipped peaks of hills I cannot see.

I cannot see the wild birds on the wing,
    But I can hear the swallows in the eaves;
I hear the song that nature has to sing—
    The gentle music of the rustling leaves.

I cannot see the children going by,
    But I can hear their laughter as they pass;
I cannot see the sunset in the sky,
    But I can feel the swaying of the grass.

I cannot see the moonlight on the sea,
  But I can hear the waves beat on the shore;
I feast upon all nature's melody
  And thank my God and do not ask for more.

NORMAN V. PEARCE

WISHES

Some may wish for city streets, jewels or silken gown;
Some may crave unbounded wealth, fame or beauty's crown;
Some may long for sunny paths that lure the pleasure bent—
But simpler things by far than these would keep my soul
    content.
A bit of God's green country, with the blue sky overhead;
A tiny shack, white curtained; on the sill, a posy red;
A laughing, chubby baby, playing inside on the floor,
And a little flower garden, growing near the open door.
A table set for supper, fresh fruit and honeycomb,
Little breezes whispering, "Your man's acomin' home."
Simple things, with love and faith—far from worldly strife,
God granting these, before I die, I'd ask no more of life.

A. C. CHILD

ON CITY STREETS

There have been times when on a city street
  Where I had seen not any face I know,
The eyes of some met mine as if to greet
  Me with a friendly word, a mute "hello."

But each is bound by laws of etiquette;
  We may not speak the words our lips would say;
So we pass on with faces firmly set—
  We fear to change the old, established way.

MARGARET E. BRUNER

ACCEPT MY FULL HEART'S THANKS

Your words came just when needed.
Like a breeze,
Blowing and bringing from the wide salt sea
Some cooling spray, to meadow scorched with heat
And choked with dust and clouds of sifted sand
That hateful whirlwinds, envious of its bloom,
Had tossed upon it. But the cool sea breeze
Came laden with the odors of the sea
And damp with spray, that laid the dust and sand
And brought new life and strength to blade and bloom
So words of thine came over miles to me,

Fresh from the mighty sea, a true friend's heart,
And brought me hope, and strength, and swept away
The dusty webs that human spiders spun
Across my path. Friend—and the word means much—
So few there are who reach like thee, a hand
Up over all the barking curs of spite
And give the clasp, when most its need is felt,
Friend, newly found, accept my full heart's thanks.

ELLA WHEELER WILCOX

THE DREADED TASK

I found the task that I had dreaded so
  Was not so difficult when once begun;
It was the dread itself that was the foe,
  And dread once conquered means a victory won.

MARGARET E. BRUNER

WHAT MAKES A HOME?

"What makes a home?"
I asked my little boy,
And this is what he said,
"You, mother,
And when father comes.
Our table set all shiny,
And my bed,
And mother, I think it's home,
Because we love each other."

You who are old and wise,
What would you say
If you were asked the question?
Tell me, pray.

And simply as a little child,
The old wise ones can answer nothing more—
A man, a woman and a child,
Their love,
Warm as the gold hearth fire along the floor.
A table, and a lamp for light.
And smooth white beds at night.
Only the old sweet fundamental things.

And long ago I learned—
Home may be near, home may be far
But it is anywhere
That love
And a few plain household treasures are.

AUTHOR UNKNOWN

The PROFIT factor is of course fundamental to the operation of any business. Certainly no business endeavor can very long survive without taking in more than goes out. In these times, however, the profit motive seems so often to out-distance and over-ride all other considerations. Graciousness, old-fashioned courtesy, service for its own sake—these are often overlooked in the search for profit or gain. GOOD DEEDS have their place in every plan, occupation and work.

BEYOND THE PROFIT OF TODAY

Lord, give me vision that shall see
　Beyond the profit of today
Into the years which are to be,
　That I may take the larger, wiser way.

I seek for fortune, Lord, nor claim
　To scorn the recompense I earn;
But help me, as I play the game,
　To give the world its just return.

Thou mad'st the earth for all of us,
　Teach me through struggle, strain and stress
To win and do my share, for thus
　Can profit lead to happiness.

Guard me from thoughts of little men
　Which blind the soul to greater things;
Save me from smug content and then
　From greed and selfishness it brings.

Aid me to join that splendid clan
　Of Business Men who seek to trace
A calm, considered working-plan
　To make the world a better place.

Teach me to hold this task above
All lesser thoughts within my ken,
That thus I may be worthy of
The name of Business Man; Amen!

AUTHOR UNKNOWN

*We fall to rise, are baffled to fight better. . . . Sickness
may afflict us, losses weaken us, disgrace and ruin overwhelm
us. Though we be unable to overcome these ills, indeed, are
overborne by them, we must prove the more the strength
and valor of our spirits. Who knows when the battle is lost?
By our endurance of the worst that life brings us we may
emerge triumphant over fate and win the victory.*

COURAGE TO LIVE

To those who have tried and seemingly have failed,
   Reach out, dear Lord, and comfort them today;
For those whose hope has dimmed, whose faith has paled,
   Lift up some lighted heavenly torch, I pray.
They are so frightened, Lord; reach out a hand.
   They are so hurt and helpless; be their friend.
Baffled and blind, they do not understand—
   They think this dark and tangled road the end.

Oh, touch to flame their hope that has burned low,
  And strike with fire faith's ashes that are dead.
Let them walk proudly once again, and go
  Seeking the sure and steadfast light ahead.
Help them to move among their fellow men
With courage to live, courage to try again.

GRACE NOLL CROWELL

MEDIATION No. 908

MEDIATORS

Dr. Frank Kingdon—*Nationally Syndicated Newspaper Columnist*

Dr. Walter B. Pitkin—*Author "Life Begins at Forty"*

Mr. George Gordon Battle—*Civic Leader; Attorney*

A type of case which has often confronted me is that of the man "who has made a mistake," who is convinced, since the cards are stacked against him, that he is, as he puts it, "all washed up." I recall a brave young wife in conflict with her husband over this defeatist attitude, which he could not or would not overcome. Eleven years before the two had married after a most pleasing romance dating back to the time they had been childhood sweethearts. During the first four years of the marriage two children were born to them. The husband was employed as the manager of the book-keeping department of the local bank, and it would have been difficult to find in their community a happier little family or one that lived a more conventional life. Four years after the marriage the wife and the younger child contracted pneumonia and were confined for a considerable period to the hospital. With the relatives of the couple in a distant section of the country, it was necessary to retain a nurse to care for the child at home, adding to the rather considerable hospital expense that had already taxed the husband's modest salary. He began to brood over his ill luck and, with time hanging heavily on his hands, sought to relieve his restlessness and uneasiness. The rest was the old story. He got in with the wrong crowd, took to drinking, gambled in the desperate hope that he would be able to win enough to keep his home going during this emergency but succeeded only in losing heavily and getting into debt. In desperation he manipulated the books, hoping to be able to make good the amounts embezzled before his crime was discovered. In all he misappropriated four thousand dollars.

The wife returned from the hospital and, taking in the situation which she attributed to the expense undergone, proceeded to effect every economy possible. She of course had no intimation of the serious trouble into which he had gotten himself.

One day to her astonishment two detectives entered the home while the reunited family was at dinner and arrested the husband. He was tried and convicted of embezzlement and sentenced to the penitentiary for the minimum term. Following the initial shock and the continued denial and suffering during his period of imprisonment, the wife welcomed him back, eager to start a new life with him, confident that he would apply himself conscientiously toward piecing together his shattered life.

At the time this case was heard the man had been out three years. In presenting the situation the wife claimed that the husband was continually throwing up the fact that there were "two strikes on him," that once a man is a "jailbird" he is forever a marked man, that it was impossible for him to "come back." Every night he came home a little more discouraged, blaming his ill luck on the impossibility of getting anywhere with a prison record. The wife attempted in vain to overcome this attitude of mind. The man insisted to the board that his experience had proven to him that it was virtually impossible to lift this "black cloud" from over his head.

I am frank to say that whenever I encountered a case of this kind it was more than a little disconcerting. Surely it does not take very long for a man such as this to sink into the quagmire of despondency. Repeated attempts, no job, no encouragement, and he becomes so broken, so filled with despair, as to be incompetent ever to rescue himself. Few employers will give a job to a man who has been involved criminally. In this particular instance the effect of the mediation was such as to enlist a tremendous public interest, and jobs from over a hundred reliable sources were offered. The additional openings were made available to others in similar situations. Today this man and his family are completely rehabilitated, and to look at him one would never know that he had been through so despairing an episode. Lifted up by this experience, he made the most of the opportunity

presented, discovered reserves of character he never real-
ized he possessed, found for himself and his family new
avenues of happiness.

The poem I read on the occasion of this broadcast was
inspired by the utterance of a well-known manufacturer to
a man who approached him for a job and started to tell his
story of having been in the penitentiary. "Never mind," said
the famous industrialist; "I don't care about the past. *Start
where you stand.*"

START WHERE YOU STAND

Start where you stand and never mind the past;
    The past won't help you in beginning new;
If you have left it all behind at last
    Why, that's enough, you're done with it, you're through;
This is another chapter in the book;
    This is another race that you have planned;
Don't give the vanished days a backward look;
    Start where you stand.

The world won't care about your old defeats
    If you can start anew and win success;
The future is your time, and time is fleet
    And there is much of work and strain and stress;
Forget the buried woes and dead despairs;
    Here is a brand-new trial right at hand;
The future is for him who does and dares;
    Start where you stand.

Old failures will not halt, old triumphs aid;
  Today's the thing, tomorrow soon will be;
Get in the fight and face it unafraid,
  And leave the past to ancient history;
What has been, has been; yesterday is dead
  And by it you are neither blessed nor banned;
Take courage, man, be brave and drive ahead;
  Start where you stand.

BERTON BRALEY

What was his creed?
I do not know his creed, I only know
That here below, he walked the common road
And lifted many a load, lightened the task,
Brightened the day for others toiling on a weary way:
This, his only meed; I do not know his creed.

.   .   .   .

His creed? I care not what his creed;
Enough that never yielded he to greed,
But served a brother in his daily need;
Plucked many a thorn and planted many a flower;
Glorified the service of each hour;
Had faith in God, himself, and fellow-men;—
Perchance he never thought in terms of creed,
I only know he lived a life, in deed!

FROM "HE LIVED A LIFE" BY H. N. FIFER

TEMPER

When I have lost my temper I have lost my reason, too.
I'm never proud of anything which angrily I do.
When I have talked in anger and my cheeks were flaming
        red,
I have always uttered something which I wish I hadn't said.
In anger I have never done a kindly deed or wise,
But many things for which I felt I should apologize.
In looking back across my life, and all I've lost or made,
I can't recall a single time when fury ever paid.
So I struggle to be patient, for I've reached a wiser age;
I do not want to do a thing or speak a word in rage.
I have learned by sad experience that when my temper flies
I never do a worthy thing, a decent deed or wise.

AUTHOR UNKNOWN

ESSAY ON MAN

Man never knows precisely what is right;
    So torn between a purpose and a doubt,
He first makes windows to let in the light
    And then hangs curtains up to shut it out.

ERASERS

Erasers are the nicest things!
  Of that there is no doubt.
We write wrong words. A few quick swipes—
  And big mistakes fade out.
And you will find erasers,
  Of a very different kind,
Extremely helpful, if you will try
  To bear these facts in mind:
When you bump someone in a crowd,
  And almost knock her down,
A soft "I'm sorry!" may bring smiles
  And rub out that old frown.
Apologies, invariably,
  Obliterate mistakes;
And three small words, "I love you!"
  Can erase the worst heartaches.

                    AUTHOR UNKNOWN

THE NEW LEAF

He came to my desk with a quivering lip;
  The lesson was done;
"Dear Teacher, I want a new leaf," he said,
  "I have spoiled this one."

I took the old leaf, torn and blotted,
And gave him a new one, all unspotted,
  And into his sad eyes smiled:
  "Do better now, my child!"

I came to the Throne with a trembling heart;
  The year's work was done;
"Dear Father, I want a new year," I said,
  "I have spoiled this one."
He took the old year, torn and blotted,
And gave me a new one, all unspotted,
  And into my sad heart smiled:
  "Do better now, my child!"

HELEN FIELD FISCHER

THIS PRAYER I MAKE

    This prayer I make,
Knowing that Nature never did betray
The heart that loved her; 'tis her privilege,
Through all the years of this our life, to lead
From joy to joy: for she can so inform
The mind that is within us, so impress
With quietness and beauty, and so feed
With lofty thoughts, that neither evil tongues,
Rash judgments, nor the sneers of selfish men,
Nor greetings where no kindness is, nor all

The dreary intercourse of daily life,
Shall e'er prevail against us, or disturb
Our cheerful faith, that all which we behold
Is full of blessings.

WILLIAM WORDSWORTH

ON WORK

Then a ploughman said, Speak to us of Work.

And (the Prophet) answered, saying:

You work that you may keep pace with the earth and the soul of the earth.

For to be idle is to become a stranger unto the seasons, and to step out of life's procession, that marches in majesty and proud submission towards the infinite.

When you work you are a flute through whose heart the whispering of the hours turns to music.

Which of you would be a reed, dumb and silent, when all else sings together in unison?

Always you have been told that work is a curse and labour a misfortune.

But I say to you that when you work you fulfil a part of earth's furthest dream . . .

And all work is empty save when there is love;

And what is it to work with love?

It is to weave the cloth with threads drawn from your heart, even as if your beloved were to wear that cloth.

It is to build a house with affection, even as if your beloved were to dwell in that house.

It is to sow seeds with tenderness and reap the harvest with joy, even as if your beloved were to eat the fruit.

It is to charge all things you fashion with a breath of your own spirit,

Work is love made visible.

And if you cannot work with love but only with distaste, it is better that you should leave your work and sit at the gate of the temple and take alms of those who work with joy.

For if you bake bread with indifference, you bake a bitter bread that feeds but half man's hunger.

And if you grudge the crushing of the grapes, your grudge distils a poison in the wine.

And if you sing though as angels, and love not the singing, you muffle man's ears to the voices of the day and the voices of the night.

FROM *The Prophet* BY KAHLIL GIBRAN

ABRIDGED

THE HUMAN TOUCH

'Tis the human touch in this world that counts,
  The touch of your hand and mine,
Which means far more to the fainting heart
  Than shelter and bread and wine;
For shelter is gone when the night is o'er,
  And bread lasts only a day,
But the touch of the hand and the sound of the voice
  Sing on in the soul alway.

SPENCER MICHAEL FREE

If we give love and sympathy
Even to those who hate us
We fill them so with mystery
They know not how to rate us.

HELEN KING

FORGET THEE?

"Forget thee?"—If to dream by night and muse on thee by
  day,
If all the worship, deep and wild, a poet's heart can pay,
If prayers in absence breathed for thee to Heaven's
  protecting power,
If winged thoughts that flit to thee—a thousand in an hour,
If busy Fancy, blending thee with all my future lot—
If this thou call'st "forgetting," thou, indeed, shalt be forgot!

FROM "FORGET THEE?" BY JOHN MOULTRIE

My soul, sit thou a patient looker-on;
Judge not the play before the play is done;
Her plot hath many changes; every day
Speaks a new scene; the last act crowns the play.

FRANCIS QUARLES

MANY THINGS

O, there be many things
    That seem right fair, below, above;
But sure not one among them all
    Is half so sweet as love.

        OLIVER WENDELL HOLMES

THERE IS A MYSTIC BORDERLAND

There is a mystic borderland that lies
Just past the limits of our workday world,
And it is peopled with the friends we met
And loved a year, a month, a week or day,
And parted from with aching hearts, yet knew
That through the distance we must loose the hold
Of hand with hand, and only clasp the thread
Of memory. But still so close we feel this land,
So sure we are that these same hearts are true,
That when in waking dreams there comes a call
That sets the thread of memory aglow,
We know that just by stretching out the hand
In written word of love, or book, or flower,
The waiting hand will clasp our own once more
Across the distance, in the same old way.

        HELEN FIELD FISCHER

WILL

There is no chance, no destiny, no fate,
Can circumvent or hinder or control
The firm resolve of a determined soul.
Gifts count for nothing; will alone is great;
All things give way before it, soon or late.
What obstacle can stay the mighty force
Of the sea-seeking river in its course,
Or cause the ascending orb of day to wait?
Each wellborn soul must win what it deserves.
Let the fool prate of luck. The fortunate
Is he whose earnest purpose never swerves,
Whose slightest action or inaction serves
The one great aim. Why, even Death stands still,
And waits an hour sometimes for such a will.

ELLA WHEELER WILCOX

A SMILE

A smile costs nothing but gives much—
It takes but a moment, but the memory of it usually lasts
    forever.
None are so rich that can get along without it—
And none are so poor but that can be made rich by it.
It enriches those who receive

Without making poor those who give—
It creates sunshine in the home,
Fosters good will in business
And is the best antidote for trouble—
And yet it cannot be begged, borrowed or stolen, for it is of
    no value
Unless it is freely given away.
Some people are too busy to give you a smile—
Give them one of yours—
For the good Lord knows that no one needs a smile so badly
As he or she who has no more smiles left to give.

AUTHOR UNKNOWN

FROM THE FLORENCE NIGHTINGALE PLEDGE

I solemnly pledge myself before God, and in the presence of this assembly, to pass my life in purity, and to practice my profession faithfully. I will do all in my power to maintain and elevate the standard of my profession, and will hold in confidence all personal matters committed to my keeping and all family affairs coming to my knowledge in the practice of my calling. With loyalty will I endeavor to aid the physician in his work, and devote myself to the welfare of those committed to my care.

TO BE A NURSE

To be a nurse is
To walk with God
Along the path that
The Master trod;
To soothe the achings
Of human pain,
To faithfully serve
For little gain.
To lovingly do
The kindly deed,
A cup of water
To one in need.
A tender hand on
A fevered brow,
A word of cheer to
The living now;
To teach the soul through
Its body's woe,
Ah! this is the way
The Lord would go.
O white-capped girls in
Dresses of blue,
The great Physician
Is working through you!

A. H. LAWRENCE

THIS, TOO, SHALL PASS AWAY

In times of trial an old Indian legend has given me much comfort. A king, who suffered many hours of discouragement, urged his courtiers to devise a motto, short enough to be engraved on a ring, which should be suitable alike in prosperity and in adversity. After many suggestions had been rejected his daughter offered an emerald bearing the inscription in Arabic, "This, too, will pass."
Said the poet:

Whate'er thou art, where'er thy footsteps stray,
   Heed these wise words: This, too, shall pass away.
Oh, jewel sentence from the mine of truth!
   What riches it contains for age or youth.
No stately epic, measured and sublime,
   So comforts, or so counsels, for all time
As these few words. Go write them on your heart
   And make them of your daily life a part.
Art thou in misery, brother? Then I pray
   Be comforted! Thy grief shall pass away.
Art thou elated? Ah, be not too gay;
   Temper thy joy; *this, too,* shall pass away.
Fame, glory, place and power,
   They are but little baubles of the hour.

Thus, be not o'er proud,
  Nor yet cast down; judge thou aright;
When skies are clear, expect the cloud;
  In darkness, wait the coming light;
Whatever be thy fate today,
  Remember, *even this*, shall pass away!

Adapted by Mr. Alexander from sources including Paul Hamilton
Hayne, John Godfrey Saxe, Ella Wheeler Wilcox.

'TIS A LITTLE JOURNEY

'Tis a little journey
  This we walk;
Hardly time for murmurs—
  Time for talk.

Yet we learn to quarrel
  And to hate;
Afterward regret it
  When too late.

Now and then 'tis sunshine—
  Sometimes dark;
Sometimes care and sorrow
  Leave their mark.

Yet we walk the pathway
  Side by side;
Where so many others
  Lived and died.

We can see the moral,
  Understand;
Yet we walk not always
  Hand in hand.

Why must there be hatred?
  Greed and strife?
Do we need such shadows
  Here in life?

AUTHOR UNKNOWN

TODAY

Today, whatever may annoy,
The word for me is Joy, just simple joy:
The joy of life;
The joy of children and of wife;
The joy of bright, blue skies;
The joy of rain; the glad surprise
Of twinkling stars that shine at night;
The joy of winged things upon their flight;
The joy of noonday, and the tried
True joyousness of eventide;
The joy of labor, and of mirth;
The joy of air, and sea, and earth—
The countless joys that ever flow from Him
Whose vast beneficence doth dim
The lustrous light of day,
And lavish gifts divine upon our way.

Whate'er there be of Sorrow
I'll put off till Tomorrow,
And when Tomorrow comes, why then
'Twill be Today and Joy again!

JOHN KENDRICK BANGS

NIGHTFALL

I need so much the quiet of your love
After the day's loud strife;
I need your calm all other things above
After the stress of life.

I crave the haven that in your dear heart lies,
After all toil is done,
I need the star shine of your heavenly eyes,
After the day's great sun.

CHARLES HANSON TOWNE

GOOD THOUGHTS

Good thoughts are the threads
With which we weave the web of life;
The threads which build
The strong and fibrous cloth
We know as character.
And, like the patterns,

That looms of modern science weave,
Our lives can be no lovelier,
No stronger, than the threads
From which our lives are made.

KATHERINE MAURINE HAAFF

NEW FRIENDS AND OLD FRIENDS

Make new friends, but keep the old;
Those are silver, these are gold.
New-made friendships, like new wine,
Age will mellow and refine.
Friendships that have stood the test—
Time and change—are surely best;
Brow may wrinkle, hair grow gray;
Friendship never knows decay.
For 'mid old friends, tried and true,
Once more we our youth renew.
But old friends, alas! may die;
New friends must their place supply.
Cherish friendship in your breast—
New is good, but old is best;
Make new friends, but keep the old;
Those are silver, these are gold.

JOSEPH PARRY

IF I KNEW YOU AND YOU KNEW ME

If I knew you and you knew me—
  If both of us could clearly see,
And with an inner sight divine
  The meaning of your heart and mine—
I'm sure that we would differ less
  And clasp our hands in friendliness;
Our thoughts would pleasantly agree
  If I knew you and you knew me.

If I knew you and you knew me,
  As each one knows his own self, we
Could look each other in the face
  And see therein a truer grace.
Life has so many hidden woes,
  So many thorns for every rose;
The "why" of things our hearts would see,
  If I knew you and you knew me.

NIXON WATERMAN

HIGH RESOLVE

I'll hold my candle high, and then
Perhaps I'll see the hearts of men
Above the sordidness of life,
Beyond misunderstandings, strife.

Though many deeds that others do
Seem foolish, rash and sinful too,
Just who am I to criticize
What I perceive with my dull eyes?
I'll hold my candle high, and then,
Perhaps I'll see the hearts of men.

AUTHOR UNKNOWN

A MORNING PRAYER

Let me today do something that will take
  A little sadness from the world's vast store,
And may I be so favored as to make
  Of joy's too scanty sum a little more.

Let me not hurt, by any selfish deed
  Or thoughtless word, the heart of foe or friend.
Nor would I pass unseeing worthy need,
  Or sin by silence when I should defend.

However meager be my worldly wealth,
  Let me give something that shall aid my kind—
A word of courage, or a thought of health
  Dropped as I pass for troubled hearts to find.

Let me tonight look back across the span
  'Twixt dawn and dark, and to my conscience say—
Because of some good act to beast or man—
  "The world is better that I lived today."

ELLA WHEELER WILCOX

*We fall to rise—are baffled—to fight better. The honorable
end—this is the one thing that cannot be taken from a man.*

THE BROKEN SWORD

This I beheld, or dreamed it in a dream:
There spread a cloud of dust along a plain;
And underneath the cloud, or in it, raged
A furious battle, and men yelled, and swords
Shocked upon swords and shields. A prince's banner
Wavered, then staggered backward, hemmed by foes.
A craven hung along the battle's edge
And thought, "Had I a sword of keener steel—
That blue blade that the king's son bears—but this
Blunt thing!" He snapt and flung it from his hand,
And lowering, crept away and left the field.
Then came the king's son, wounded, sore bestead,
And weaponless, and saw the broken sword,
Hilt-buried in the dry and trodden sand,
And ran and snatched it, and with battle shout
Lifted afresh he hewed his enemy down,
And saved a great cause that heroic day.

EDWARD ROWLAND SILL

LEST THOU FORGET

Lest thou forget in the years between
The beautiful things thine eyes have seen:
The light of the sun and the silver sheen
Of cobwebs over a field of green . . .

The birth of love on a destined day
When blossomed the first sweet flowers of May
And sunlight flooded the wistful way;

The vows we took and the prayers we said
When the urge of love to the altars led
And the mystical marriage rites were read;

The sacrament scenes of death and birth;
The tragedies testing human worth—
These are the timeless things of earth!

Reverence, worship, and love and prayer,
Kneeling alone at the altar stair,
Hearing the Infinite whisper there.

WILLIAM L. STIDGER

ON FILE

If an unkind word appears,
  File the thing away.
If some novelty in jeers,
  File the thing away.
If some clever little bit
Of a sharp and pointed wit,
Carrying a sting with it—
  File the thing away.

If some bit of gossip come,
  File the thing away.
Scandalously spicy crumb,
  File the thing away.
If suspicion comes to you
That your neighbor isn't true
Let me tell you what to do—
  File the thing away.

Do this for a little while,
Then go out and burn the file.

                      JOHN KENDRICK BANGS

THE FAMILY

So blest are they who round a family board
May gather:—May they humbly thank the Lord,
Not only for the food they common share,
But for the dear, loved faces circled there:
So oft, unless we face that board alone,
We treasure not its true, sweet sense of home.

So blest are they, when low the pale stars ride,—
If cheer, and warmth, and welcome safe abide
Within their shelter. Patient they would grow,—
Kinder,—more understanding,—could they know
How empty is the house where no glad light
Shines from its windows, out upon the night.

So blest are they who have within their home
That touch of kinship,—folks they call their own,—
Flesh of their flesh: Ah, how they'd earnest strive
To ease small tensions, keeping love alive,
If once they knew the desolate despair
That haunts the house with no one waiting there.

DONNA R. LYDSTON

THE MOST VITAL THING IN LIFE

When you feel like saying something
  That you know you will regret,
Or keenly feel an insult
  Not quite easy to forget,
That's the time to curb resentment
  And maintain a mental peace,
For when your mind is tranquil
  All your ill-thoughts simply cease.

It is easy to be angry
  When defrauded or defied,
To be peeved and disappointed
  If your wishes are denied;
But to win a worthwhile battle
  Over selfishness and spite,
You must learn to keep strict silence
  Though you know you're in the right.

So keep your mental balance
  When confronted by a foe,
Be it enemy in ambush,
  Or some danger that you know.
If you are poised and tranquil
  When all around is strife,
Be assured that you have mastered
  The most vital thing in life.

                GRENVILLE KLEISER

MEDIATION No. 11009

Rt. Rev. Francis J. McConnell—*Bishop of the Methodist Church, New York*
Hon. Edward Corsi—*Commissioner of Labor, State of New York*
Mr. Edwin S. Friendly—*Vice-President, American Association of Newspaper Publishers*

One need not be a philosopher to know that there are two things which monopolize the interest of most people in this life—one is love; the other is money. It is particularly unfortunate when the craving for money so warps one's sense of values as to intrude upon what could probably be a fine and sincere relationship. Especially is this unfortunate when the relationship is that of husband and wife.

He was an architect, she an advertising copy writer. They had been married for twelve years, and there was one child. Because of a series of misunderstandings over money, resulting in a mutual lack of trust, the husband abruptly departed from the home. At the time the wife came to the board he had been absent for about three months. It appears that for several years she had regularly turned over her salary check to him to be deposited in a joint account from which neces-

sary household expenses were deducted. When the wife dis-
covered that her husband was not depositing his income
regularly but was making investments, she discontinued the
practice of giving him her check, opening up for the first
time a personal account. The husband felt this step unwar-
ranted, since it was his contention that his manipulations
were in their mutual interest. He stated that until such time
as she could see things differently and resume depositing
her salary in the joint account, he would withhold his earn-
ings entirely. He then made his departure. In the meantime
the woman was beside herself. Deeply in love with her hus-
band, she was, nevertheless, in dread fear that if she did as
instructed he would one day take all the money and leave
her destitute. Incidentally, she was not a well woman.

In the consideration of this case it was emphasized that
so many estrangements in marriage come about because of
conditions of poverty. It was regrettable that in this instance
the earning power of both parties and their good fortune
economically had served to bring about bitterness and an-
tagonism instead of a sense of well-being and gratitude for
whatever blessings they had. The board was constrained to
hold that this marital arrangement had developed into a
commercial proposition rather than a marriage and in-
structed the respondent husband that his persistent refusal
to return to the home was hardly conducive to bringing
about an amicable settlement, that he could hardly expect
his wife to have confidence in him unless he indicated by
his general attitude that it was his desire to live with her in
a state of peace and harmony. It was agreed that there was
not even the slightest chance for this marriage unless the

husband sought to win his wife's affection by acts of kind-
ness rather than by threats not to return.

As it turned out, the husband moved back to the home,
but the damage had already been done. His repentance
came just a little late, for a few months later the wife, her
illness aggravated by the situation, passed away at the age
of thirty-one, leaving a seven-year-old child. The husband
realizes now that "money isn't everything."

The evening the issue was submitted to the board by both
parties to the conflict, I concluded the hour with the poem,
Better Than Gold.

BETTER THAN GOLD

Better than grandeur, better than gold,
Than rank and titles a thousandfold,
Is a healthy body and a mind at ease,
And simple pleasures that always please.
A heart that can feel for another's woe,
And share his joys with a genial glow;
With sympathies large enough to enfold
All men as brothers, is better than gold.

Better than gold is a conscience clear,
Though toiling for bread in an humble sphere,
Doubly blessed with content and health,
Untried by the lusts and cares of wealth,

Lowly living and lofty thought
Adorn and ennoble a poor man's cot;
For mind and morals in nature's plan
Are the genuine tests of an earnest man.

Better than gold is a peaceful home
Where all the fireside characters come,
The shrine of love, the heaven of life,
Hallowed by mother, or sister, or wife.
However humble the home may be,
Or tried with sorrow by heaven's decree,
The blessings that never were bought or sold,
And center there, are better than gold.

ABRAM J. RYAN

THE DOOR-BELL

I never hear it ring without
    A creepy little thrill
Expectant of some possible
    Adventure, good or ill.

It may be just a friend who comes
    To have a cup of tea;
It may be just a letter's old
    Familiar mystery.

It may be one who comes to sell
    Some queer, unwanted thing;
Or one who brings the latest news
    Of war and uncrowned king.

It may be just these happenings
  Of every-day, but still
I never hear it ring without
  That funny little thrill.

CHARLOTTE BECKER

DISILLUSION

Suppose some of the hopes we cherished have not stood
the test of trial. Our house of dreams has tumbled. Perhaps
it was reared, not on the rock of reality but on the sands of
unreality. Disillusionment comes because we were dealing
with illusions. But now, we are fortunate enough to know
the truth. We see things as they are. Which means that our
life today is infinitely sounder, saner, safer than it was be-
fore, when the way only seemed so smooth beneath our
feet. If we understand it rightly, disillusion can be the cor-
rective of illusion and thus understood, it may do for us
what David tried to do for Saul, in Browning's poem,

> ". . . *bid (us) awake*
> *From the dream . . . to find (ourselves) set*
> *Clear and safe in new light and new life."*

Who looking back upon his troubled years
  Can say he has not gained through sorrow's rain
Something of good? For through his falling tears
  He sees the storms have vanished with their pain

Leaving him nobler, cut in finer mold;
  Made strong by conflict, purified by fire
To leave the grains of gold;
  The soul is freed forevermore from strife
And enters into rich abundant life.

BESSIE B. DECKER

THE NIGHT HAS A THOUSAND EYES

The night has a thousand eyes,
  And the day but one;
Yet the light of the bright world dies
  With the dying sun.

The mind has a thousand eyes,
  And the heart but one;
Yet the light of a whole life dies
  When its love is done.

FRANCIS W. BOURDILLON

THERE IS A MYSTERY IN HUMAN HEARTS

There is a mystery in human hearts,
And though we be encircled by a host
Of those who love us well and are beloved,
To every one of us, from time to time,

There comes a sense of utter loneliness.
Our dearest friend is "stranger" to our joy,
And cannot realize our bitterness.
"There is no one who really understands,
No one to enter into all I feel";
Such is the cry of each of us in turn
We wander in "a solitary way."
No matter what or where our lot may be,
Each heart, mysterious even to itself,
Must live its inner life in solitude.
And would you know the reason why this is?
It is because the Lord desires our love,
In every heart He wishes to be first,
He therefore keeps the secret key himself,
To open all its chambers and to bless
With perfect sympathy and holy peace,
Each solitary soul which comes to Him.
And when beneath some heavy cross you faint,
And say, "I cannot bear this load alone," you say the truth.
God made it purposely
So heavy that you must return to Him,
The bitter grief, which "no one understands,"
Conveys a secret message from the king,
Entreating you to come to Him again.
You cannot come too often or too near.
The God of Mercy is infinite in grace,
His presence satisfies the longing soul
And those who walk with Him from day to day
Can never have "a solitary way."

AUTHOR UNKNOWN

ONE YEAR TO LIVE

If I had but one year to live;
One year to help; one year to give;
One year to love; one year to bless;
One year of better things to stress;
One year to sing; one year to smile;
To brighten earth a little while;
I think that I would spend each day,
In just the very self-same way
That I do now. For from afar
The call may come to cross the bar
At any time, and I must be
Prepared to meet eternity.
So if I have a year to live,
Or just a day in which to give
A pleasant smile, a helping hand,
A mind that tries to understand
A fellow-creature when in need,
'Tis one with me,—I take no heed;
But try to live each day He sends
To serve my gracious Master's ends.

MARY DAVIS REED

TRUE LOVE

I think true love is never blind,
  But rather brings an added light,
An inner vision quick to find
  The beauties hid from common sight.

No soul can ever clearly see
  Another's highest, noblest part;
Save through the sweet philosophy
  And loving wisdom of the heart.

Your unanointed eyes shall fall
  On him who fills my world with light;
You do not see my friend at all;
  You see what hides him from your sight.

I see the feet that fain would climb;
  You but the steps that turn astray;
I see the soul, unharmed, sublime;
  You, but the garment and the clay.

You see a mortal, weak, misled,
  Dwarfed ever by the earthly clod;
I see how manhood, perfected,
  May reach the stature of a god.

Blinded I stood, as now you stand,
  Till on mine eyes, with touches sweet,
Love, the deliverer, laid his hand,
  And lo! I worship at his feet!

PHOEBE CARY

WHAT SHALL I DO?

What shall I do with all the days and hours
That must be counted ere I see thy face?
How shall I charm the interval that lowers
Between this time and that sweet time of grace?

. . . .

Oh, how, or by what means, may I contrive
To bring the hour that brings you back more near?
How may I teach my drooping hopes to live
Until the blessed time that thou art here?

. . . .

FROM "ABSENCE" BY FRANCES ANNE KEMBLE

DUSK

These are the things men seek at dusk:
  Firelight across a room,
Green splashing against dim roofs,
  Gardens where flowers bloom.
Lamplighted gold of a windowpane,

Trees with tall stars above,
Women who watch a darkening street
    For somebody they love.
Faith of a small child's rhyming prayer,
    Candle shine . . . tables spread
With a blossom or two in a gay blue bowl,
    Fragrance of crusted bread.
For men may dream of a clipper ship,
    A wharf or a gypsy camp,
But their footsteps pattern a homing way
    To a woman, a child, a lamp.

                    HELEN WELSHIMER

For age is opportunity no less
Than youth itself, though in another dress,
And as the evening twilight fades away
The sky is filled with stars, invisible by day.

              FROM "MORITURI SALUTAMUS"
        BY HENRY WADSWORTH LONGFELLOW

PARTING

If thou dost bid thy friend farewell,
But for one night though that farewell may be,
Press thou his hand in thine.
How canst thou tell how far from thee

Fate or caprice may lead his steps ere that tomorrow comes?
Men have been known to lightly turn the corner of a street,
And days have grown to months, and months to lagging
    years,
Ere they have looked in loving eyes again.
Parting, at best, is underlaid
With tears and pain.
Therefore, lest sudden death should come between,
Or time, or distance, clasp with pressure firm
The hand of him who goeth forth;
Unseen, Fate goeth too.
Yes, find thou always time to say some earnest word
Between the idle talk,
Lest with thee henceforth,
Night and day, regret should walk.

COVENTRY PATMORE

GIVING AND FORGIVING

What makes life worth the living
    Is our giving and forgiving;
Giving tiny bits of kindness
    That will leave a joy behind us,
And forgiving bitter trifles
    That the right word often stifles,
For the little things are bigger
    Than we often stop to figure.
What makes life worth the living
    Is our giving and forgiving.

THOMAS GRANT SPRINGER

IF I CAN STOP ONE HEART FROM BREAKING

If I can stop one heart from breaking,
　I shall not live in vain;
If I can ease one life the aching,
　Or cool one pain,
Or help one lonely person
　Into happiness again
I shall not live in vain.

EMILY DICKINSON

TRIBUTE ON THE PASSING OF A VERY REAL PERSON

People are of two kinds, and he
Was the kind I'd like to be.
Some preach their virtues, and a few
Express their lives by what they do;
That sort was he. No flowery phrase
Or glibly spoken word of praise
Won friends for him. He wasn't cheap
Or shallow, but his course ran deep,
And it was pure. You know the kind.
Not many in life you find
Whose deeds outrun their words so far
That more than what they seem, they are.

AUTHOR UNKNOWN

THOSE WE LOVE THE BEST

One great truth in life I've found,
    While journeying to the West——
The only folks we really wound
    Are those we love the best.

The man you thoroughly despise
    Can rouse your wrath, 'tis true;
Annoyance in your heart will rise
    At things mere strangers do.

But those are only passing ills;
    This rule all lives will prove;
The rankling wound which aches and thrills
    Is dealt by hands we love.

The choicest garb, the sweetest grace,
    Are oft to strangers shown;
The careless mien, the frowning face,
    Are given to our own.

We flatter those we scarcely know,
    We please the fleeting guest,
And deal full many a thoughtless blow
    To those we love the best. . . .

ELLA WHEELER WILCOX

You wake up in the morning, and lo! your purse is magically filled with twenty-four hours of the magic tissue of the universe of your life. No one can take it from you. No one receives either more or less than you receive. Waste your infinitely precious commodity as much as you will, and the supply will never be withheld from you. Moreover, you cannot draw on the future. Impossible to get into debt. You can only waste the passing moment. You cannot waste tomorrow; it is kept for you.

ARNOLD BENNETT

SOMEWHERE

Somewhere there waiteth in this world of ours
    For one lone soul, another lonely soul—
Each chasing each through all the weary hours,
    And meeting strangely at one sudden goal;
Then blend they—like green leaves with golden flowers,
    Into one beautiful and perfect whole—
And life's long night is ended, and the way
    Lies open onward to eternal day.

SIR EDWIN ARNOLD

FAITH

I will not doubt, though all my ships at sea
   Come drifting home with broken masts and sails;
   I shall believe the Hand which never fails,
From seeming evil worketh good to me;
   And, though I weep because those sails are battered,
   Still will I cry, while my best hopes lie shattered,
      "I trust in Thee."

I will not doubt, though all my prayers return
   Unanswered from the still, white realm above;
   I shall believe it is an all-wise Love
Which has refused those things for which I yearn;
   And though, at times, I cannot keep from grieving,
   Yet the pure ardor of my fixed believing
      Undimmed shall burn.

I will not doubt, though sorrows fall like rain,
   And troubles swarm like bees about a hive;
   I shall believe the heights for which I strive,
Are only reached by anguish and by pain;
   And, though I groan and tremble with my crosses,
   I yet shall see, through my severest losses,
      The greater gain.

I will not doubt; well anchored in the faith,
   Like some stanch ship, my soul braves every gale,
   So strong its courage that it will not fail

To breast the mighty, unknown sea of death.
Oh, may I cry when body parts with spirit,
"I do not doubt," so listening worlds may hear it
With my last breath.

ELLA WHEELER WILCOX

A little work, a little play
To keep us going—and so, good-day!

A little warmth, a little light
Of love's bestowing—and so, good-night!

A little fun, to match the sorrow
Of each day's growing—and so, good-morrow!

A little trust, that when we die
We reap our sowing! and so—*good-bye!*

AUTHOR UNKNOWN

PRAYER FOR STRENGTH

Though I should be maligned by those
I trust, let not my spirit be
Broken and bowed, but may the throes
Of suffering set me free

From pettiness and that desire
  Which goads one to retaliate;
With patience I would quench the fire
  Of vengeance, ere it be too late.

And in defeat may I cast out
  The moods of envy and despair,
And from my heart, Lord, I would rout
  All bitterness. This is my prayer.

MARGARET E. BRUNER

*"Two men look out through the same bars
One sees the mud, and one the stars."*

THE PESSIMIST

The pessimist's a cheerless man;
  To him the world's a place
Of anxious thoughts and clouds and gloom;
  Smiles visit not his face.

Though brightest sunshine floods the earth,
  And flowers are all ablow,
He spreads depression where he can
  By dismal tales of woe.

The pessimist's a hopeless man,
  He's full of doubt and fear;
No radiant visions come to him
  Of glad days drawing near.

The pessimist's a joyless man,
  He finds no sweet delight
In making this a happier world,
  In fighting for the right.

He views the future with alarm,
  He sees no light ahead;
Most wretched of all men is he,
  Because his hope is dead.

AUTHOR UNKNOWN

HOW TO FORGET

If you were busy being kind,
Before you knew it, you would find
You'd soon forget to think 'twas true
That someone was unkind to you.

If you were busy being glad
And cheering people who are sad,
Although your heart might ache a bit,
You'd soon forget to notice it.

If you were busy doing good,
And doing just the best you could,
You'd not have time to blame some man
Who's doing just the best he can.

If you were busy being right,
You'd find yourself too busy quite
To criticize your neighbor long
Because he's busy being wrong.

REBECCA FORESMAN

LIFE'S MIRROR

There are loyal hearts, there are spirits brave,
There are souls that are pure and true,
Then give the world the best you have,
And the best will come back to you.

Give love, and love to your life will flow,
A strength in your utmost need,
Have faith, and a score of hearts will show
Their faith in your word and deed.

Give truth, and your gift will be paid in kind;
And honor will honor meet;
And a smile that is sweet will surely find
A smile that is just as sweet.

Give pity and sorrow to those who mourn,
You will gather in flowers again
The scattered seeds from your thought outborne
Though the sowing seemed but vain.

For life is the mirror of king and slave,
'Tis just what we are and do;
Then give to the world the best you have,
And the best will come back to you.

MADELINE BRIDGES

"ARE YOU THERE?"

I like to play close by my father's den,
Where he's at work, and every now and then
Ask: "Father, are you there?" He answers back:
"Yes, son." That time I broke my railroad track
All into bits, he stopped his work and came
And wiped my tears, and said, "Boy, boy! Be game!"
And then he showed me how to fix it right,
And I took both my arms and hugged him tight.

Once, when I'd asked him if he still was there,
He called me in and rumpled up my hair,
And said: "How much alike are you and I!
When I feel just as boys feel when they cry,
I call to our Big Father, to make sure
That He is there, my childish dread to cure.
And always, just as I to you, 'Yes, son';
Our Father calls, and all my fret is done!"

STRICKLAND GILLILAN

SONG

Love that is hoarded, moulds at last
  Until we know some day
The only thing we ever have
  Is what we give away.

And kindness that is never used
  But hidden all alone
Will slowly harden till it is
  As hard as any stone.

It is the things we always hold
  That we will lose some day;
The only things we ever keep
  Are what we give away.

               HAROLD C. SANDALL

THE ANVIL—GOD'S WORD

Last eve I passed beside a blacksmith's door,
And heard the anvil ring the vesper chime;
Then, looking in, I saw upon the floor
Old hammers, worn with beating years of time.

"How many anvils have you had," said I,
"To wear and batter all these hammers so?"
"Just one," said he, and then with twinkling eye,
"The anvil wears the hammers out, you know."

And so, thought I, the anvil of God's Word,
For ages skeptic blows have beat upon;
Yet, though the noise of falling blows was heard,
The anvil is unharmed—the hammers gone.

AUTHOR UNKNOWN

CRIME AND PUNISHMENT

. . . Ofttimes have I heard you speak of one who commits a
wrong as though he were not one of you, but a stranger
unto you and an intruder upon your world.

But I say that even as the holy and the righteous can-
not rise beyond the highest which is in each one of you,
So the wicked and the weak cannot fall lower, than the
lowest which is in you also . . .

. . . And if any of you would punish in the name of right-
eousness and lay the ax unto the evil tree, let him see to
its roots;
And verily he will find the roots of the good and the
bad, the fruitful and the fruitless, all entwined together
in the silent heart of the earth . . .

FROM *The Prophet* BY KAHLIL GIBRAN

No man is an island, entire of itself; every man is a piece of the continent, a part of the main; . . . any man's death diminishes me, because I am involved in mankind; and therefore *never send to know for whom the bell tolls;* IT TOLLS FOR THEE.

FROM *Devotions XVII* BY JOHN DONNE

"Shut-ins," we say, as we envision that multitude in the confines of quiet rooms, in hospital cots, or in wheel chairs, are set apart from their fellows. Withdrawn from the active arena of human beings, their share in the vital work of the world seems over. For them there is only the gray prospect of loneliness, pain, suffering, trying days and sleepless nights. And yet the handicap may be only of the body. In so many cases, the ministry of suffering has yielded a wealth of spiritual experience that has flowed out in freshening streams to enrich the world.

"Shut-in," we say; yes, that the busy, hurrying throng of humanity may pause for a while by these quiet "sanctuaries" and, entering in, behold the inner radiance of the soul.

THE SHUT-IN

She lives a prisoner within
  The four bare walls of her poor room.
In the bright world she walks no more,
  Yet cheerfully accepts her doom.

And holds that Life is very sweet,
  As eagerly she looks and sees
The golden sunlight daily creep
  Into her room, and with it weaves

Fantastic dreams of rosy hue;
  Delightful things—in which she sees
The sparkling earth bedecked with dew—
  Green hills and vales and stately trees.

She lives a prisoner—and yet,
  She gets more out of life than we
Who walk bowed down with care—and fret
  For things we are too blind to see.

                  NELLIE DE HEARN

WORTH WHILE

It is easy enough to be pleasant,
　　When life flows by like a song,
But the man worth while is one who will smile,
　　When everything goes dead wrong.
For the test of the heart is trouble,
　　And it always comes with the years,
And the smile that is worth the praises of earth
　　Is the smile that shines through tears.

It is easy enough to be prudent,
　　When nothing tempts you to stray,
When without or within no voice of sin
　　Is luring your soul away;
But it's only a negative virtue
　　Until it is tried by fire,
And the life that is worth the honor on earth
　　Is the one that resists desire.

By the cynic, the sad, the fallen,
　　Who had no strength for the strife,
The world's highway is cumbered today;
　　They make up the sum of life.
But the virtue that conquers passion,
　　And the sorrow that hides in a smile,
It is these that are worth the homage on earth
　　For we find them but once in a while.

ELLA WHEELER WILCOX

WHEN A MAN TURNS HOMEWARD

When a man turns homeward through the moonfall,
Swift in his path like a meteor bright,
Kindling his wonder and blinding his sight,
His feet will go on, his heartbeats will call
Deep in his breast like quick music, and all
The darkness that swirls like a flame of dead light
Cannot fetter his feet turned homeward at night.
Past thicket and trees like a towering wall
He will go on over hillside and stone,
Clinging like hope to the road that he knows;
Groping along like a shadow, alone,
He will reach for the latch where a candle, gold-eyed,
Watches with her for the door that will close,
Leaving the world like a kitten outside!

                              DANIEL WHITEHEAD HICKY

MEDIATION No. *1894*

MEDIATORS

Col. Gilbert T. Hodges—*President American Association of Advertising Agencies*
Dr. Ira S. Wile—*Psychiatrist*
Mr. Lloyd Paul Stryker—*Attorney*

Two sisters, both employed and supporting an elderly mother and father, complained that a brother, twenty-eight years old, refused to shoulder any of the family responsibilities, was simply satisfied to live at home, "sponge" on the family, enjoy himself as a gentleman of leisure, without recognizing the existence of any obligation. Since this condition had prevailed for many years and was becoming worse, they felt the time had come when something must be done.

The young man gave as his excuse the usual one about economic conditions today and the difficulty of obtaining decent employment, but the sisters had good reason to feel that in his case the matter was simply one of laziness, that the brother was quite satisfied to continue as he was, as long as he had a home and three meals a day. After considerable questioning it was conceded by the callous young man that since he hadn't asked to come into the world he failed to

see any special obligation to worry—that the future some-
how had a habit of taking care of itself. It was the feeling
of the two girls that they had been more than tolerant with
him, since practically all of the money they earned went
toward the upkeep of the family and home, not to speak
of his maintenance. Because of this extra burden they were
forced to scrimp on such clothes as a girl might want and
forgo even moderate pleasures. They saw no end to the
situation and were concerned as to the future.

As a result of the mediation the young man (who had
been spoiled in earlier years by an overindulgent mother
and who had never looked upon himself as a parasite) be-
gan to see the picture somewhat more clearly. He managed
to get himself a job, and if not an active contributor, he is
now at least self-sustaining and considerably more self-re-
specting. The poem read on the occasion of the hearing of
this case seemed especially appropriate.

TWO KINDS OF PEOPLE

There are two kinds of people on earth today,
Just two kinds of people, no more, I say,
Not the good and the bad, for 'tis well understood
The good are half bad and the bad are half good.

Not the happy and sad, for the swift flying years
Bring each man his laughter and each man his tears.
Not the rich and the poor, for to count a man's wealth
You must first know the state of his conscience and health.

Not the humble and proud, for in life's busy span
Who puts on vain airs is not counted a man.
No! The two kinds of people on earth I mean
Are the people who lift, and the people who lean.

Wherever you go you will find the world's masses
Are ever divided in just these two classes.
And, strangely enough, you will find, too, I wean,
There is only one lifter to twenty who lean.

This one question I ask. Are you easing the load
Of overtaxed lifters who toil down the road?
Or are you a leaner who lets others bear
Your portion of worry and labor and care?

ELLA WHEELER WILCOX

THE SIN OF OMISSION

It isn't the thing you do;
    It's the thing you leave undone,
Which gives you a bit of heartache
    At the setting of the sun.

The tender word forgotten,
    The letter you did not write,
The flower you might have sent,
    Are your haunting ghosts tonight.

The stone you might have lifted
   Out of a brother's way,
The bit of heartsome counsel
   You were hurried too much to say.

The loving touch of the hand,
   The gentle and winsome tone,
That you had no time or thought for
   With troubles enough of your own.

The little acts of kindness,
   So easily out of mind;
Those chances to be helpful
   Which everyone may find—

No, it's not the thing you do,
   It's the thing you leave undone,
Which gives you the bit of heartache
   At the setting of the sun.

                    MARGARET E. SANGSTER

AT A WINDOW

Give me hunger,
O you gods that sit and give
The world its orders.
Give me hunger, pain and want;
Shut me out with shame and failure
From your doors of gold and fame,
Give me your shabbiest, weariest hunger.

But leave me a little love;
A voice to speak to me in the day-end,
A hand to touch me in the dark room,
Breaking the long loneliness.
In the dusk of day-shapes,
Blurring the sunset,
One little wandering, western star
Thrust out from the changing shores of shadow.
Let me go to the window,
Watch there the day-shapes of dusk,
And wait and know the coming
Of a little love.

CARL SANDBURG

DEFINITIONS

"Honor," said the man,
"is character, immaculate
belief, integrity.
Honor is holding one's name
as the sun by day,
as a star by night,
as a candle if dark creeps
into the heart or mind.

Honor is the immeasurable
pride of man, the forward striving
of man toward immortality,
the impeccable fruition."

"Honor," said the child,
"is never telling another,
and never telling yourself
a lie."

JOSEPH JOEL KEITH

PAIN

Why must I be hurt?
Suffering and despair,
Cowardice and cruelty,
Envy and injustice,
All of these hurt.
Grief and terror,
Loneliness and betrayal
And the agony of loss or death—
All these things hurt.
Why? Why must life hurt?
Why must those who love generously,
Live honorably, feel deeply
All that is good—and beautiful
Be so hurt,
While selfish creatures
Go unscathed?
That is why—
Because they can feel.
Hurt is the price to pay for feeling.
Pain is not accident,
Nor punishment, nor mockery

By some savage god.
Pain is part of growth.
The more we grow
The more we feel—
The more we feel—the more we suffer,
For if we are able to feel beauty,
We must also feel the lack of it—
Those who glimpse heaven
Are bound to sight hell.
To have felt deeply is worth
Anything it cost.
To have felt Love and Honor,
Courage and Ecstasy
Is worth—any price.
And so—since hurt is the price
Of Larger living, I will not
Hate pain, nor try to escape it.
Instead I will try to meet it
Bravely, bear it proudly:
Not as a cross, or a misfortune, but an
Opportunity, a privilege, a challenge—to the God that
gropes within me.

ELSIE ROBINSON

HYMN

When winds are raging o'er the upper ocean,
    And billows wild contend with angry roar,
'Tis said, far down beneath the wild commotion,
    That peaceful stillness reigneth, evermore.

Far, far beneath, the noise of tempests dieth,
And silver waves chime ever peacefully,
And no rude storm, how fierce soe'er it flieth,
Disturbs the Sabbath of that deeper sea.

HARRIET BEECHER STOWE

FIRST IMPRESSIONS

It is not right to judge a man
    By hasty glance or passing whim,
Or think that first impressions can
    Tell all there is to know of him.

Who knows what weight of weariness
    The man we rashly judge may bear,
The burden of his loneliness.
    His blighted hopes, his secret care.

A pompous guise or air of pride
    May only be an outward screen,
A compensation meant to hide
    A baffled will, a grief unseen.

However odd a person seems,
    However strange his ways may be,
Within each human spirit gleams
    A spark of true divinity.

So what can first impressions tell?
  Unthinking judgments will not do,
Who really knows a person well
  May also come to *like* him too!

ALFRED GRANT WALTON

THIS IS YOUR HOUR

This is your hour—creep upon it!
Summon your power, leap upon it!
Grasp it, clasp it, hold it tight!
Strike it, spike it, with full might!
If you take too long to ponder,
Opportunity may wander.
Yesterday's a bag of sorrow;
No man ever finds Tomorrow.
Hesitation is a mire—
Climb out, climb up, climb on higher!
Fumble, stumble, risk a tumble,
Make a start, however humble!
Do your best and do it now!
Pluck and grit will find out how.
Persevere, although you tire—
While a spark is left, there's fire.
Distrust doubt; doubt is a liar.
Even if all mankind jeer you,
You can force the world to cheer you.

HERBERT KAUFMAN

GOOD IN EVERYTHING

And this our life, exempt from public haunt,
Finds tongues in trees, books in the running brooks,
Sermons in stones, and good in every thing.

FROM "AS YOU LIKE IT" BY WILLIAM SHAKESPEARE

THE OLD YEAR

What is the old year? 'Tis a book
On which we backward fondly look,
Not willing, quite, that it should close,
For leaves of violet and rose
Within its heart are thickly strewn,
Marking Love's dawn and golden noon;
And turned-down pages, noting days
Dimly recalled through Memory's haze;
And tear-stained pages, too, that tell
Of starless nights and mournful knell
Of bells that toll through troubled air
The *De Profundis* of despair;
The laugh, the tear, the shine, the shade,
All 'twixt the covers gently laid,
No leaves uncut, no page unscanned—
Close it and lay it in God's hand.

CLARENCE URMY

THE NEW YEAR

A flower unblown; a book unread;
A tree with fruit unharvested;
A path untrod; a house whose rooms
Lack yet the heart's divine perfumes:
A landscape whose wide border lies
In silent shade, 'neath silent skies;
A treasure with its gifts concealed—
This is the year that for you waits
Beyond tomorrow's mystic gates.

HORATIO NELSON POWERS

FATE

Two shall be born, the whole wide world apart,
And speak in different tongues and have no thought
Each of the other's being, and no heed;
And these, o'er unknown seas, to unknown lands
Shall cross, escaping wreck, defying death;
And all unconsciously shape every act
And bend each wandering step to this one end—
That one day out of darkness they shall meet
And read life's meaning in each other's eyes.

190

And two shall walk some narrow way of life
So nearly side by side that, should one turn
Ever so little space to left or right,
They needs must stand acknowledged, face to face,
And yet, with wistful eyes that never meet,
And groping hands that never clasp, and lips
Calling in vain to ears that never hear,
They seek each other all their weary days
And die unsatisfied—and this is Fate!

SUSAN MARR SPALDING

PATIENCE WITH THE LIVING

Sweet friend, when you and I are gone
    Beyond earth's weary labor,
When small shall be our need of grace
    From comrade or from neighbor,
Then hands that would not lift a stone,
    Where stones were thick to cumber
Our steep hill path, will scatter flowers
    Above our pillowed slumber.

Sweet friend, perchance both thou and I,
    Ere love is past forgiving,
Should take the earnest lesson home—
    Be patient with the living.
Today's repressed rebuke may save
    Our blinding tears tomorrow.
Then patience, e'en when keenest edge
    May whet a nameless sorrow.

'Tis easy to be gentle when
   Death's silence shames our clamor,
And easy to discern the best
   Through memory's mystic glamour;
But wise it were for thee and me,
   Ere love is past forgiving,
To take the earnest lesson home—
   Be patient with the living.

                MARGARET E. SANGSTER

A DAY

What does it take to make a day?
A lot of love along the way:
It takes a morning and a noon,
A father's voice, a mother's croon;
It takes some task to challenge all
The powers that a man may call
His own: the powers of mind and limb;
A whispered word of love; a hymn
Of hope—a comrade's cheer—
A baby's laughter and a tear;
It takes a dream, a hope, a cry
Of need from some soul passing by;
A sense of brotherhood and love;
A purpose sent from God above;
It takes a sunset in the sky,
The stars of night, the winds that sigh;

It takes a breath of scented air,
A mother's kiss, a baby's prayer.
That is what it takes to make a day:
A lot of love along the way.

WILLIAM L. STIDGER

PRAYER OF ANY HUSBAND

Lord, may there be no moment in her life
When she regrets that she became my wife,
And keep her dear eyes just a trifle blind
To my defects, and to my failings kind!

Help me to do the utmost that I can
To prove myself her measure of a man,
But, if I often fail as mortals may,
Grant that she never sees my feet of clay!

And let her make allowance—now and then—
That we are only grown-up boys, we men,
So, loving all our children, she will see,
Sometimes, a remnant of the child in me!

Since years must bring to all their load of care,
Let us together every burden bear,
And when Death beckons one its path along,
May not the two of us be parted long!

MAZIE V. CARUTHERS

SUCCESS

Genius, that power which dazzles mortal eyes,
Is oft but perseverance in disguise.
Continuous effort of itself implies,
In spite of countless falls, the power to rise.
'Twixt failure and success the print's so fine,
Men sometimes know not when they touch the line;
Just when the pearl is waiting one more plunge,
How many a struggler has thrown up the sponge!
As the tide goes clear out it comes clear in;
In business 'tis at turns, the wisest win;
And, oh, how true when shades of doubt dismay,
" 'Tis often darkest just before the day."
A little more persistence, courage, vim,
Success will dawn o'er failure's cloudy rim.
Then take this honey for the bitterest cup;
There is no failure, save in giving up.
No real fall, so long as one still tries,
For seeming set-backs make the strong man wise.
There's no defeat, in truth, save from within;
Unless you're beaten there, you're bound to win.

C. C. CAMERON

SPEAK GENTLY

Speak gently; it is better far
 To rule by love than fear;
Speak gently; let no harsh word mar
 The good we may do here.

Speak gently to the little child;
 Its love be sure to gain;
Teach it in accents soft and mild;
 It may not long remain.

Speak gently to the young; for they
 Will have enough to bear;
Pass through this life as best they may,
 'Tis full of anxious care.

Speak gently to the aged one.
 Grieve not the careworn heart;
Whose sands of life are nearly run,
 Let such in peace depart.

Speak gently, kindly to the poor,
 Let no harsh tone be heard;
They have enough they must endure,
 Without an unkind word.

Speak gently to the erring; know
　　They must have toiled in vain;
Perchance unkindness made them so;
　　Oh, win them back again.

Speak gently; Love doth whisper low
　　The hearts that true hearts bind.
And gently Friendship's accents flow;
　　Affection's voice is kind.

Speak gently; 'tis a little thing
　　Dropped in the heart's deep well;
The good, the joy that it may bring,
　　Eternity shall tell.

G. W. LANGFORD

HOME

Home to me is laughter . . .
Kisses on my cheek when they're least expected;
Glances filled with gladness;
The happiness in knowing
I'm a portion of
My family's fulfillment.
Home to me . . . is love!

JUNE BROWN HARRIS

LITTLE THINGS

Little words are the sweetest to hear; little charities fly farthest, and stay longest on the wing; little lakes are the stillest; little hearts are the fullest, and little farms are the best tilled. Little books are read the most, and little songs the dearest loved. And when Nature would make anything especially rare and beautiful, she makes it little; little pearls, little diamonds, little dews. Agar's is a model prayer; but then it is a little one; and the burden of the petition is for but little. The Sermon on the Mount is little, but the last dedication discourse was an hour long. Life is made up of littles; death is what remains of them all. Day is made up of little beams, and night is glorious with little stars.

LIFE'S MADE UP OF LITTLE THINGS

Life's made up of little things,
no great sacrifice or duty,
but smiles and many a cheerful word
fill up our lives with beauty.

The heartaches, as they come and go,
are but blessings in disguises,
for time will turn the pages o'er
and show us great surprises.

MARY R. HARTMAN

PRAYER

Lord, make me an instrument of Thy Peace.
Where there is hatred, let me sow love.
Where there is injury, pardon.
Where there is doubt, faith.
Where there is despair, hope.
Where there is darkness, light.
Where there is sadness, joy.

O Divine Master, grant that I may not so much seek to be
consoled as to console; to be understood, as to understand;
to be loved, as to love; for it is in giving that we receive, it
is in pardoning that we are pardoned, and it is in dying
that we are born to Eternal Life.

ST. FRANCIS OF ASSISI

WE HAVE LIVED AND LOVED TOGETHER

We have lived and loved together
  Through many changing years;
We have shared each other's gladness
  And wept each other's tears;
I have known ne'er a sorrow
  That was long unsoothed by thee;
For thy smiles can make a summer
  Where darkness else would be.

Like the leaves that fall around us
    In autumn's fading hours,
Are the traitor's smiles, that darken
    When the cloud of sorrow lowers;
And though many such we've known, love,
    Too prone, alas, to range,
We both can speak of one love
    Which time can never change.

We have lived and loved together
    Through many changing years;
We have shared each other's gladness
    And wept each other's tears.
And let us hope the future
    As the past has been will be:
I will share with thee my sorrows,
    And thou thy joys with me.

                          CHARLES JEFFERYS

YOUR NEIGHBOR

Do you know the neighbor who lives in your block;
Do you ever take time for a bit of a talk?
Do you know his troubles, his heartaches, his cares,
The battles he's fighting, the burdens he bears?
Do you greet him with joy or pass him right by
With a questioning look and a quizzical eye?
Do you bid him "Good morning" and "How do you do,"
Or shrug up as if he was nothing to you?

He may be a chap with a mighty big heart,
And a welcome that grips, if you just do your part.
And I know you'll coax out his sunniest smile,
If you'll stop with this neighbor and visit awhile.

We rush on so fast in these strenuous days,
We're apt to find fault when it's better to praise.
We judge a man's worth by the make of his car;
We're anxious to find what his politics are.
But somehow it seldom gets under the hide,
The fact that the fellow we're living beside
Is a fellow like us, with a hankering, too,
For a grip of the hand and a "How do you do!"
With a heart that responds in a welcome sincere
If you'll just stop to fling him a message of cheer,
And I know you'll coax out his sunniest smile,
If you'll stop with this neighbor and visit awhile.

H. HOWARD BIGGAR

THE BEGGAR

The day was one of weariness
    With no bright interlude;
I was fatigued by homely tasks—
    Bereft of fortitude.

Night's shadows brought a deeper gloom
    And when a sudden knock
Upon the door came startling me,
    Trembling, I turned the lock.

There stood a tired, dejected man
  Who humbly asked for bread,
And in his countenance there was
  No thing to fear or dread.

For meekness and humility
  Were stamped upon his face
As though some sorrow's heavy weight
  Had passed and left its trace.

Forgetting care, I turned to fetch
  A plate of meat and bread;
By serving him somehow my heart
  Was strangely comforted.

And evil tales of vagrant folk
  All vanished when he said:
"I thank you for this kindly act,"
  Then bowed and trudged ahead. . . .

Did he know that I too had begged
  But not for earthly bread—
That when I gave him food and drink
  My spirit had been fed?

                    MARGARET E. BRUNER

GOOD-BY

Good-by can be a happy word
  When lightly spoken,
As if a carefree heart conferred
  A trifling token.

But when we part from those held dear
  The voice grows tender;
We smile to hide the unwelcome tear
  And scorn surrender.

Hands clasped and seeing eye to eye,
  All else unheeding,
How sacred is the word good-by,
  Like suppliants pleading.

                    MARGARET E. BRUNER

THE LITTLE THINGS

Men cannot guess the things they do
To make a woman feel secure
And loved. The merest well-timed smile
Can stir her heart and leave it sure.

A man may slave to prove his faith
And never dream, that has not meant
So much to her at watching him
Just smoke a pipe at home, content.

The loud, protective ways of men
Are there for all the world to see
But women warm their hearts as fires
That burn unnoticed, quietly.

ELIZABETH ISLER

The holiest of all holidays are those
Kept by ourselves in silence and apart;
The secret anniversaries of the heart.

FROM "HOLIDAYS"
BY HENRY WADSWORTH LONGFELLOW

SILENCE

I have known the silence of the stars and of the sea,
And the silence of the city when it pauses,
And the silence of a man and a maid.
And the silence for which music alone finds the word,
And the silence of the woods before the winds of spring
   begin,
And the silence of the sick
When their eyes roam about the room.

And I ask: For the depths
Of what use is language?
A beast of the fields moans a few times
When death takes its young.
And we are voiceless in the presence of realities—
We cannot speak.

A curious boy asks a soldier
Sitting in front of the general store,
"How did you lose your leg?"
And the soldier is struck with silence,
Or his mind flies away
Because he cannot concentrate it on Tarawa.
And there are no words—
No words.
And the boy wonders, while the soldier
Dumbly, feebly lives over
The flashes of guns, the thunder of bombs,
The shrieks of the slain,
And himself lying on the ground,
And the hospital surgeons, the knives,
And the long days in bed.
But if he could describe it all
He would be an artist.
But if he were an artist there would be deeper wounds
Which he could not describe.

There is a silence of a great hatred,
And the silence of a great love,
And the silence of a deep peace of mind
And the silence of an embittered friendship,

There is the silence of a spiritual crisis,
Through which your soul, exquisitely tortured
Comes with visions not to be uttered
Into a realm of higher life.
And the silence of the gods who understand each other
   without speech,
There is the silence of the defeated
There is the silence of those unjustly punished;
And the silence of the dying whose hand
Suddenly grips yours.
There is the silence between father and son,
When the father cannot explain his life,
Even though he be misunderstood for it.

There is the silence that comes between husband and wife.
There is the silence of those who have failed;
And the vast silence that covers
Broken nations and vanquished leaders.
There was the silence of Lincoln,
Thinking of the poverty of his youth.
And a silence of Napoleon
After Waterloo.
And a silence of Joan of Arc
Saying amid the flames, "Blessed Jesus"—
Revealing in two words all sorrow, all hope.
And there is the silence of age,
Too full of wisdom for the tongue to utter it
In words intelligible to those who have not lived
The great range of life.
The temple of our purest thoughts—*Is silence*.

EDGAR LEE MASTERS

THE HATE AND THE LOVE OF THE WORLD

I have seen men binding their brothers in chains, and crafty
    traders reaching for the bread that women and children
    lifted to their mouths;
I have seen suffering go unaided.
I have heard the iron din of war, and have seen the waxen
    face of early death;
And I have cried in my heart, "The world is hate!"

I have heard birds calling their mates in the still forests,
    and insects chirping to their loves in the tangled grass
    of meadows;
I have seen mothers caressing their babes, and aged men
    supporting with devotion the slow steps of stooping
    women;
I have seen cheerful hearthstones surrounded by laughing
    children and strong men and happy women;
I have heard the tender words of lovers in the pure passion
    of youth;
And I have cried in my heart, "The world is love!"

MAX EHRMANN

WHO ARE MY PEOPLE?

My people? Who are they?
I went into the church where the congregation
Worshiped my God. Were they my people?
I felt no kinship to them as they knelt there.
My people! Where are they?
I went into the land where I was born,
Where men spoke my language . . .
I was a stranger there.
"My people," my soul cried. "Who are my people?"

Last night in the rain I met an old man
Who spoke a language I do not speak,
Which marked him as one who does not know my God
With apologetic smile he offered me
The shelter of his patched umbrella.
I met his eyes . . . And then I knew. . . .

ROSA ZAGNONI MARINONI

Talk not of strength, till your heart has known
And fought with weakness through long hours alone.

Talk not of virtue, till your conquering soul
Has met temptation and gained full control.

Boast not of garments, all unscorched by sin,
Till you have passed unscathed through fires within.

AUTHOR UNKNOWN

PRAISE

Praise is a quiet and a gracious thing,
Like buds slow-forming, where the woods are bare,
Or silent recognition of the spring
Waiting to break upon the tremulous air.
  Praise is a pillow to the tired head,
  A lamp to light the traveler on his way;
  It's the generous sacrament of bread
  Shared between strangers at the close of day.
Swift is the word of praise to soothe the smart
Of old defeats, to light the troubled face;
Sweeter, oh, sweeter to the thirsty heart
Than streams of water in a desert place!

R. H. GRENVILLE

The thoughtful word of encouragement that may be of use in teaching us—not so much what we are—but what we can, and ought to be.

OLD HOUSES

There is comfort in old houses,
  Like a mother's arm, or a friend's kind words.
There is joy in time-scarred timbers,
  In slated roofs and weathered boards.
    (I am one with an old house:
     I am one with its pains and joys:
    An old house shared the travail of my mother.
    An old house shared my baby toys.)

Old houses have a blessed look,
  That is one with God's great plan.
Old houses have a tenderness,
  From the baby's crawl to the stride of the man.
    (I am one with an old house,
     I am one with its kind embrace
    An old house shared my mother's love
    An old house knew my mother's lovely face.)

HOMER D'LETTUSO

IN YOUR ABSENCE

It may be when the sunlight strikes the sill
A certain way. Your hand once rested there,
And so, remembering that, my heart stands still,
As one who has been running stops for air.
Or in a crowd some friend may say your name,
Or just a name that's similar to yours,
And all my pulses leap as leaps a flame
When someone adds a twig. These are your lures.
The snares your hand and voice have set for me
Are many as the things I hear and see.

ELIZABETH BAXTER

LITTLE THINGS

There's nothing very beautiful and nothing very gay
About the rush of faces in the town by day,
But a light tan cow in a pale green mead,
That is very beautiful, beautiful indeed. . . .
And the soft March wind, and the low March mist
Are better than kisses in a dark street kissed. . . .
The fragrance of the forest when it wakes at dawn,
The fragrance of a trim green village lawn,
The hearing of the murmur of the rain at play—
These things are beautiful, beautiful as day!

And I shan't stand waiting for love or scorn
When the feast is laid for a day new born. . . .
Oh, better let the little things I loved when little
Return when the heart finds the great things brittle;
And better is a temple made of bark and thong
Than a tall stone temple that may stand too long.

ORRICK JOHNS

We may live without poetry, music and art;
We may live without conscience and live without heart;
We may live without friends; we may live without books;
But civilized man can not live without cooks.
He may live without books,—what is knowledge but griev-
    ing?
He may live without hope,—what is hope but deceiving?
He may live without love,—what is passion but pining?
But where is the man that can live without dining?

OWEN MEREDITH

QUIET DAYS

The gentle, cheerful ticking of a clock;
A cloud that moves in leisurely pursuit;
The slow erosion of an ageless rock;
The timeless roar of sea that is not mute;
The patient building of a hill by ants;

The laboured steps before a child can walk;
The months when baby's words are chirps and chants,
Before he has acquired the skill of talk—
These made me wonder at my restless haste,
But it was illness that taught me to know
That quiet days are not a barren waste;
Though one lies still, the heart and mind can grow.

MILDRED T. MEY

THE SHIP THAT SAILS

I'd rather be the ship that sails
    And rides the billows wild and free;
Than to be the ship that always fails
    To leave its port and go to sea.

I'd rather feel the sting of strife,
    Where gales are born and tempests roar;
Than to settle down to useless life
    And rot in dry dock on the shore.

I'd rather fight some mighty wave
    With honor in supreme command;
And fill at last a well-earned grave,
    Than die in ease upon the sand.

I'd rather drive where sea storms blow,
  And be the ship that always failed.
To make the ports where it would go,
  Than be the ship that never sailed.

AUTHOR UNKNOWN

THE BLIND MEN AND THE ELEPHANT

It was six men of Indostan
  To learning much inclined,
Who went to see the elephant
  (Though all of them were blind),
That each by observation
  Might satisfy his mind.

The First approached the elephant,
  And, happening to fall
Against his broad and sturdy side,
  At once began to bawl:
"God bless me! but the elephant
  Is nothing but a wall!"

The Second, feeling of the tusk,
  Cried: "Ho! what have we here
So very round and smooth and sharp?
  To me 'tis mighty clear
This wonder of an elephant
  Is very like a spear!"

The Third approached the animal,
   And, happening to take
The squirming trunk within his hands,
   Thus boldly up and spake:
"I see," quoth he, "The elephant
   Is very like a snake!"

The Fourth reached out his eager hand,
   And felt about the knee:
"What most this wondrous beast is like
   Is mighty plain," quoth he;
"'Tis clear enough the elephant
   Is very like a tree."

The Fifth, who chanced to touch the ear,
   Said: "E'en the blindest man
Can tell what this resembles most;
   Deny the fact who can,
This marvel of an elephant
   Is very like a fan!"

The Sixth no sooner had begun
   About the beast to grope,
Than, seizing on the swinging tail
   That fell within his scope,
"I see," quoth he, "The elephant
   Is very like a rope!"

And so these men of Indostan
　　Disputed loud and long,
Each in his own opinion
　　Exceeding stiff and strong,
Though each was partly in the right,
　　And all were in the wrong!

So, oft in theologic wars
　　The disputants, I ween,
Rail on in utter ignorance
　　Of what each other mean,
And prate about an elephant
　　Not one of them has seen!

　　　　　　　　JOHN GODFREY SAXE

FOR ONE WHO IS SERENE

Sometimes when I feel hurried or dismayed,
Your face in calmness comes before my view,
And on your features then I see displayed
An understanding look, as if you knew
That I have need of your serenity;
I feel your presence though you dwell afar,
And something of your poise is given to me,
Remote, yet like a steady-gleaming star . . .
Madonna-like, it seems you are imbued
With peace, which lends me strength and fortitude.

　　　　　　　　MARGARET E. BRUNER

FAITH

"Keep this for me."
What child has not said this,
And placed a treasure in his Mother's hand
With strict injunction she should keep it safe
Till he return?
He knows with her it will be safe;
No troubled thought or anxious fear besets his mind,
And off he runs light-hearted to his play.

If children can so trust, why cannot we,
And place our treasures, too, in God's safe hand;
Our hopes, ambitions, needs, and those we love,
Just see them, in his all embracing care,
And say with joyous heart, "They are with Thee."

AUTHOR UNKNOWN

*"To have Faith—in the best and highest that we know—
is to be borne along, through the difficulties of life—as on
wings of air."*

OLD HOUSES

I like old houses, with steps that sag,
And worn picket fences running zig-zag
Like little children playing tag.
Happy old houses, with thresholds worn thin,
By young ones and old ones who walked out and in.

I like old houses, that squat in the rain,
That have welcomed the years and sheltered the pain
Of knowing they wait for a loved one in vain.
Crazy old houses that bask in the sun,
Browned like a crusty, flaky bun.

I like old houses that patiently wait,
For a new friend's hand on the creaky gate—
Knowing that love is never too late.
Houses sagacious—like prophets of old;
Knowing so many things they never have told.

JENNIE ROMANO

THANKSGIVING

Lord, behold our family here assembled. We thank Thee
for this place in which we dwell; for the love that unites
us; for the peace accorded us this day; for the hope with

which we expect the morrow; for the health, the work, the food, and the bright skies that make our lives delightful; for our friends in all parts of the earth . . .

Give us courage, gaiety, and the quiet mind. Spare to us our friends, soften to us our enemies. Bless us, if it may be, in all our innocent endeavors. If it may not, give us the strength to encounter that which is to come, that we be brave in peril, constant in tribulation, temperate in wrath, and in all changes of fortune, loyal and loving one to another.

ROBERT LOUIS STEVENSON

MEDIATION No. 2053

MEDIATORS

Rev. Dr. Harry Emerson Fosdick
Major General John F. O'Ryan—*Former Police
Commissioner, City of New York*
Gene Fowler—*Author and Playwright*

It has been said that "the souls of emperors and cobblers are cast in the same mold. The identical reason that makes us wrangle with a neighbor causes a war between kings." It is always unfortunate when people of ordinarily kind and friendly instincts are hostile toward each other due to a misunderstanding as to the sincerity and merit of each other's motives. It is indeed strange how people can go on for years without really talking matters over in a rational way and ironing them out.

In this seemingly trivial yet significant situation two property owners living in adjoining one-family houses were engaged in controversy. The complainant, a middle-aged woman who lived alone with her mother, claimed that she was constantly annoyed by the actions of her next-door neighbor, who because of his alleged dislike for her persisted in a campaign of malicious mischief. So bitter was the animosity that the police had been called by both on numerous occasions, an action which did nothing but aggravate the situation. The woman claimed that the man damaged her property, made insulting remarks about her mother as well as herself, embarrassed her in front of her company by gaping whenever they entered or left, parked his car in her driveway and, in general, interfered with the peace of mind of both her old mother and herself.

The neighbor, in pleading his cause, maintained that in the thirteen years during which he had owned his house he had at no previous time experienced difficulty with any other neighbor. He claimed that the woman was bitterly resentful because he had complained to her repeatedly about the incessant barking of her dog, which was particularly annoying since he was employed at night and was obliged to get his sleep during the day. The neighborhood in which these people resided is a suburban one, and the controversy between the two had reached such proportions as to become a matter of community gossip.

Needless to say, the willingness evidenced by these people to submit their differences was a most encouraging step toward that co-operation which is so vital in our relations with each other. The finger was placed on the causes of the irritation between them, and when it was discovered that much of the misunderstanding had been provoked by a former house employee of the man, who had carried tales to both of the parties, the picture was seen in proper perspective. As the two left, chatting amiably (the respondent inviting the complainant to drive home with him in his car), there was no doubt that they had begun to see the tremendous possibilities inherent in talking things over. The poem read that evening was entitled *The Kindly Neighbor.*

THE KINDLY NEIGHBOR

I have a kindly neighbor, one who stands
Beside my gate and chats with me awhile.
Gives me the glory of his radiant smile
And comes at times to help with willing hands.
No station high or rank this man commands;
He, too, must trudge, as I, the long day's mile;
And yet, devoid of pomp or gaudy style,
He has a worth exceeding stocks or lands.

To him I go when sorrow's at my door;
On him I lean when burdens come my way;
Together oft we talk our trials o'er,
And there is warmth in each good night we say.
A kindly neighbor! Wars and strife shall end
When man has made the man next door his friend.

EDGAR A. GUEST

HARMONY

In the far spaces of eternity
  The planets swing, each following some sun.
  In perfect rhythm, each and every one,
The singing spheres keep time to harmony.

And this, our little earth, swings with its moon
  To the sure rhythm of the Master Hand
  Whose unseen movements are Divine command
To which the silent symphony must attune.

One discord and the Universe would fall;
  One false note in the measured march of Time,
  One halt, one pause in rhythm or in rhyme,
And then wild chaos would engulf us all.

But still they move in perfect harmony,
  The near, cold moon, the farthest, unseen star;
  There is perfection in each note and bar
Of the great paeon of eternity.

Only we trivial crawlers on the earth
  Abound in discord, jangle out of tune,
  Defy the majesty of night and noon,
And mock the very symphony of birth.

But still the singing spheres swing on through space
  And heed us not, for in their harmony
  No muted echoes come from such as we—
In their grand anthem discord has no place.

                    THOMAS GRANT SPRINGER

LET US HAVE PEACE

The earth is weary of our foolish wars.
Her hills and shores were shaped for lovely things,
Yet all our years are spent in bickerings
    Beneath the astonished stars.

April by April laden with beauty comes,
Autumn by Autumn turns our toil to gain,
But hand at sword hilt, still we start and strain
    To catch the beat of drums.

Knowledge to knowledge adding, skill to skill,
We strive for others' good as for our own—
And then, like cavemen snarling with a bone,
    We turn and rend and kill. . . .

With life so fair, and all too short a lease
Upon our special star! Nay, love and trust,
Not blood and thunder shall redeem our dust.
    Let us have peace!

                    NANCY BYRD TURNER

"The only way to have a friend is to be one"
EMERSON

THE ONLY WAY TO HAVE A FRIEND

The only way to have a friend
Is to be one yourself;
The only way to keep a friend
Is to give from that wealth.

For friendship must be doublefold,
Each one must give his share
Of feelings true if he would reap
The blessings that are there.

If you would say, "He is my friend,"
Then nothing else will do
But you must say, "I am his friend,"
And prove that fact be true.

AUTHOR UNKNOWN

THE TOUCH OF HUMAN
HANDS

The touch of human hands—
That is the boon we ask;
For groping, day by day,
Along the stony way,
We need the comrade heart
That understands,
And the warmth, the living warmth
Of human hands.

The touch of human hands;
Not vain, unthinking words,
Nor that cold charity
Which shuns our misery:
We seek a loyal friend
Who understands,
And the warmth, the pulsing warmth
Of human hands. . . .

THOMAS CURTIS CLARK

ATONEMENT

How often we neglect a friend
   When living—but should death appear,
The penitent heart is quick to send
   A wreath to lay upon his bier.

MARGARET E. BRUNER

DROP A PEBBLE IN THE WATER

Drop a pebble in the water: just a splash, and it is gone;
   But there's half-a-hundred ripples circling on and on and
      on,
Spreading, spreading from the center, flowing on out to the
      sea.
   And there is no way of telling where the end is going to
      be.

Drop a word of cheer and kindness: just a flash and it is
      gone;
   But there's half-a-hundred ripples circling on and on and
      on,
Bearing hope and joy and comfort on each splashing,
      dashing wave
   Till you wouldn't believe the volume of the one kind
      word you gave.

Drop a word of cheer and kindness: in a minute you forget;
  But there's gladness still a-swelling, and there's joy
    a-circling yet,
And you've rolled a wave of comfort whose sweet music can
    be heard
    Over miles and miles of water just by dropping one kind
      word.

JAMES W. FOLEY

VISION

There have been times when I have looked at life
From out the eyes of sorrow, and have felt
The utter loneliness of black night vigils.
There have been times when I have wept hot tears
And tasted of their salt
And drunk the dregs of sadness to the end.

There have been times—and then another's heartache,
So deep and rending as to mock my own,
Has cut, flamelike, across my blurring vision,
Dwarfing my paltry tragedies to nought.

ELIZABETH N. HAUER

Grow old along with me!
The best is yet to be,
The last of life for which the first was made;
Our times are in His hand
Who saith: "A whole I planned—
Youth shows but half; trust God, see all nor be afraid."
FROM "RABBI BEN EZRA" BY ROBERT BROWNING

MEDIATION No. 13057

MEDIATORS

Dr. John Haynes Holmes—*Minister of the Community Church*
Hon. William Hodson—*Commissioner of Welfare, City of New York*
Hon. Frederick R. Coudert—*Civic Leader; Attorney*

This is a story of ingratitude that is almost unbelievable —the story of a woman who loved "not wisely but too well." She had married eighteen years before. Shortly after the ceremony the woman discovered that her husband was afflicted with a chronic nervous disease. Were it not for her love, she could have easily procured an annulment, due to his concealment from her of the nature and existence of his ailment. Instead of alienating her, however, his illness in-

227

spired a deep sense of dedication. "He needs me," she insisted, and protestations by her family to the effect that the marriage was a mistake were in vain. Such was her solicitude for his welfare and so tender her care, that she spent wakeful hours without end, endeavoring to alleviate his condition. During a considerable part of this period the man was not gainfully employed, and her accumulated savings dwindled and finally were gone.

Three years ago it was apparent that he was cured, but with the restoration of his health and his renewed capacity to take part in outside activities, he began to lose interest in his wife and benefactor. At one time most attractive, the years of the woman's hardship and anxiety had taken their toll. In any event, the day came when he began to withhold some of his salary, finally ceasing to contribute anything toward the maintenance of the home. When the issue could no longer be avoided he informed her that she was no longer attractive to him and left her. Long suffering, still devoted, the woman was anxious to forgive.

Two years after the husband's departure the matter was submitted to mediation. She loved him, weakness as well as strength; she was used to him, could find no happiness without him. During the years of her dedication she had lost the interest and affection of her family and friends, who from the beginning had disapproved of the relationship. She was virtually friendless and alone. The position of the man was simply stated. He was not happy with her. He was unable to understand why he should be forced to live with someone whom he no longer loved. She did not share his ideas of life and was anything but a good companion. In particular, she was not a well woman, was nervous and excitable. Was it reasonable to expect him to live with someone who failed to conform to his ideal of a companion? Why couldn't he live his life as he wanted to live it?

A woman past fifty, it would have been surprising, indeed, if she had been able to salvage much charm after twenty years of self neglect, only to find herself cast aside, as she put it, "like a worn-out old shoe." It was from this wife "who now got on his nerves" that the man sought escape. He readily acknowledged that his wife had been everything fine and good to him, that he had treated her shabbily, but claimed the answer could be found in the obvious fact that however much she loved him, he was simply unable to return that love.

I shall never forget the interesting and illuminating discussion that followed. Aside from the ingratitude that featured this case, it was emphasized that here was a man who had approached the whole marriage relationship from the standpoint of its service and satisfaction, who regarded his wife merely as an instrument of pleasure. By way of example one of the mediators told the story of one of the truest and happiest marriages he had ever known. After several years of marriage, suddenly, through an accident, the wife became a hopeless invalid. For years she lay broken and helpless in her bed, her mind as alert, her spirit as vigorous, as ever, but her body as helpless as a doll's. Did this make a difference in the love of this husband and wife? Yes, in the sense that their love became a thing so beautiful in its essence, so ineffable in its quality of pure spirit, that it seemed as though these two had been transformed into the guise of angels. For years the wife lived but to plot and plan for the greater happiness of her husband, and through the same years the husband went in and out of his home with only one thought—the happiness of his stricken wife.

And so it is with many true marriages, where love seems to become strengthened and purified as they move into the years.

The husband and wife who had submitted this issue for hearing left arm in arm. The next day I received in the mail a long letter from the wife. She said: "I cannot rest without first writing you. We spent last night at home together for the first time in two years. We had a wonderful talk; it was the first time he has ever been willing to discuss this thing calmly. My heart tells me that he is on the road to being a better husband. God bless you." The poem I read that memorable evening was entitled *Wedding Anniversary*.

WEDDING ANNIVERSARY

This is the anniversary of the day
　　Of days, for us, when we with faith and hope
Fared forth together; solemn and yet gay
　　We faced the future, for life's upward slope
Was joyous going, and we never thought
　　Then, that there might be worries—hours of pain
And sleepless nights that left one overwrought—
　　That loss would often come instead of gain.

But looking back, the time has not seemed long,
　　Although the road, for us, was sometimes rough . . .
We have grown quiet and the buoyant song
　　Once in our hearts sings low, and yet enough
Of loveliness still lives to make amend
　　To us, for all the ills life chose to send.

MARGARET E. BRUNER

HYMN OF MARRIAGE

The question is asked, "Is there anything more beautiful in life than a boy and girl clasping clean hands and pure hearts in the path of marriage?" And the answer is given, "Yes—there is a more beautiful thing; it is the spectacle of an old man and an old woman finishing their journey together on that path. Their hands are gnarled but still clasped; their faces are seamed but still radiant; their hearts are tired and bowed down but still strong. They have proved the happiness of marriage and have vindicated it from the jeers of cynics."

JOHN ANDERSON, MY JO

John Anderson, my jo,* John,
   When we were first acquent,
Your locks were like the raven,
   Your bonnie brow was brent;
But now your brow is beld, John,
   Your locks are like the snow;
But blessings on your frosty pow,
   John Anderson, my jo.

* "Jo" means "dear," "darling," "beloved," "sweetheart."

John Anderson, my jo, John,
  We clamb the hill thegither,
And mony a cantie day, John,
  We've had wi' ane anither:
Now we maun totter down, John,
  And hand in hand we'll go,
And sleep thegither at the foot,
  John Anderson, my jo.

ROBERT BURNS

AS WE GROW OLDER

A little more tired at close of day;
A little less anxious to have our way;
A little less ready to scold and blame;
A little more care of a brother's name;
And so we are nearing the journey's end,
Where time and eternity meet and blend.
And so we are faring adown the way
That leads to the gates of a better day.
A little more laughter, a few more tears,
And we shall have told our increasing years.
The book is closed and the prayers are said,
And we are part of the countless dead.
And so we are going, where all must go,
To the place the living may never know.
Thrice happy if then some soul can say,
"I'm better because he passed my way."

ROLLIN J. WELLS

IDEALS

Some men deem
Gold their god, and some esteem
Honor is the chief content
That to man in life is lent;
And some others do contend,
Quite none like to a friend;
Others hold there is no wealth
Compared to a perfect health;
Some man's mind in quiet stands
When he is lord of many lands:
But I did sigh, and said all this
Was but a shade of perfect bliss;
And in my thoughts I did approve
Naught so sweet as is true love.

ROBERT GREENE

ROOF-TOPS

Roof-tops, roof-tops, what do you cover?
Sad folk, bad folk, and many a glowing lover;
Wise people, simple people, children of despair—
Roof-tops, roof-tops, hiding pain and care.

Roof-tops, roof-tops, O what sin you're knowing,
While above you in the sky the white clouds are blowing.
While beneath you, agony and dolor and grim strife
Fight the olden battle, the olden war of Life.

Roof-tops, roof-tops, cover up their shame—
Wretched souls, prisoned souls too piteous to name;
Man himself hath built you all to hide away the stars—
Roof-tops, roof-tops, you hide ten million scars.

Roof-tops, roof-tops, well I know you cover
Many solemn tragedies, and many a lonely lover;
But, ah! you hide the good that lives in the throbbing city—
Patient wives, and tenderness, forgiveness, faith, and
    pity. . . .

CHARLES HANSON TOWNE

LEARN TO WAIT

Learn to wait—life's hardest lesson
    Conned, perchance, through blinding tears;
While the heart throbs sadly echo
    To the tread of passing years.
Learn to wait—hope's slow fruition;
    Faint not, though the way seems long;
There is joy in each condition;
    Hearts through suffering may grow strong.

Thus a soul untouched by sorrow
  Aims not at a higher state;
Joy seeks not a brighter morrow;
  Only sad hearts learn to wait.

AUTHOR UNKNOWN

FAITH FOR TOMORROW

"Tomorrow, friend, will be another day,"
A seer wise of old was wont to say
To him who came at eventide, in grief,
Because the day had borne no fruitful sheaf.

O Lord of Life, that each of us might learn
From vain todays and yesterdays to turn,
To face the future with a hope newborn
That what we hope for cometh with the morn!

THOMAS CURTIS CLARK

GOD BE WITH YOU

May His Counsels Sweet uphold you,
  And His Loving Arms enfold you,
    As you journey on your way.

May His Sheltering Wings protect you,
And His Light Divine direct you,
Turning darkness into day.

May His Potent Peace surround you,
And His Presence linger with you,
As your inner, golden ray.

AUTHOR UNKNOWN

THE PHILOSOPHER

I saw him sitting in his door,
Trembling as old men do;
His house was old; his barn was old,
And yet his eyes seemed new.

His eyes had seen three times my years
And kept a twinkle still,
Though they had looked at birth and death
And three graves on a hill.

"I will sit down with you," I said,
"And you will make me wise;
Tell me how you have kept the joy
Still burning in your eyes."

Then like an old-time orator
  Impressively he rose;
"I make the most of all that comes,
  The least of all that goes."

The jingling rhythm of his words
  Echoes as old songs do,
Yet this had kept his eyes alight
  Till he was ninety-two.

SARA TEASDALE

WHO LOVES THE RAIN

Who loves the rain
  And loves his home,
And looks on life with quiet eyes,
  Him will I follow through the storm;
  And at his hearth-fire keep me warm;
Nor hell nor heaven shall that soul surprise,
  Who loves the rain,
  And loves his home,
And looks on life with quiet eyes.

FRANCES WILLS SHAW

SELFISHNESS

Death takes our loved ones—
We are bowed in grief. For whom?
Are we not selfish?
A mourner weeps for himself,
The dead know nought of sorrow.

MARGARET E. BRUNER

ENDURANCE

How much the heart may bear and yet not break!
 How much the flesh may suffer and not die!
I question much if any pain or ache
 Of soul or body brings our end more nigh:
Death chooses his own time; till that is sworn,
 All evil may be borne.

. . . .

Behold, we live through all things—famine, thirst,
 Bereavement, pain, all grief and misery,
All woe and sorrow; life inflicts its worst
 On soul and body—but we cannot die,
Though we be sick, and tired, and faint and worn—
 Lo, all things can be borne!

ELIZABETH AKERS ALLEN

TALK HAPPINESS

Talk happiness. The world is sad enough
  Without your woe. No path is wholly rough;
Look for the places that are smooth and clear,
  And speak of those, to rest the weary ear
Of Earth, so hurt by one continuous strain
  Of human discontent and grief and pain.

Talk faith. The world is better off without
  Your uttered ignorance and morbid doubt.
If you have faith in God, or man, or self,
  Say so. If not, push back upon the shelf
Of silence, all your thoughts, till faith shall come;
  No one will grieve because your lips are dumb.

Talk health. The dreary, never-ending tale
  Of mortal maladies is more than stale.
One cannot charm, or interest, or please
  By harping on that minor chord, disease.
Say you are well, or all is well with you,
  And God shall hear your words and make them true.

ELLA WHEELER WILCOX

A POEM FOR CHRISTMAS

If Christmas brought me nothing more,
Than a cozy chair by the open fire,
With the children playing upon the floor,
And I with a book and a well filled briar,
Or a friend or two, just to chat awhile,
And watch the little folks at play,
Recalling, too, with a tender smile,
The joys of a bygone Christmas Day;
If I had nothing more than this,
'Twould be a day of peaceful bliss.

But Christmas joys spring not alone
From selfish comforts such as these,
And man can scarce enjoy his own,
Till he has done his best to ease
The grief and pain that, everywhere,
Abides among us, so today,
My book and pipe and easy chair,
Must wait till in my humble way,
I do the things I find to do,
To make folks happy round about,
And do them all so quiet too,
That other folks won't find it out.
Enough, I think, to more than fill
Most any soul with God's Good Will.

C. A. SNODGRASS

I THINK THAT GOD IS PROUD

I think that God is proud of those who bear
  A sorrow bravely—proud indeed of them
Who walk straight through the dark to find Him there,
  And kneel in faith to touch His garment's hem.
Oh, proud of them who lift their heads to shake
  Away the tears from eyes that have grown dim,
Who tighten quivering lips and turn to take
  The only road they know that leads to Him.

How proud He must be of them—He who knows
  All sorrow, and how hard grief is to bear!
I think He sees them coming, and He goes
  With outstretched arms and hands to meet them there,
And with a look, a touch on hand or head,
  Each finds his hurt heart strangely comforted.

GRACE NOLL CROWELL

MEDIATION No. *1313*

MEDIATORS

Hon. Edward P. Mulrooney—*Former Police
Commissioner, City of New York*
Rev. Dr. Robert J. McCracken
Hon. Paul Moss—*Commissioner, Department
of Licenses, City of New York*

There is a terrible story of a married couple who lived under the same roof for twenty-three years without speaking, because neither would break the silence with the first word of penitence. The husband and wife had shown deep evidence of love following a beautiful courtship, and the first few years of marriage were replete with mutual acts of consideration and sacrifice. One day, as it happened, there was a quarrel over some question pertaining to the wife's mother. It was a slight misunderstanding such as might often take place, and under ordinary circumstances the difference would have been adjusted easily enough.

Unfortunately, however, part of the quarrel took place within hearing of the mother, and that night she had a heart attack (which may or may not have been induced by the excitement) and died. Such sorrow has the tendency sometimes to bring people closer together, but in this case the overburdened wife inadvertently accused her mate of responsibility for her mother's death and in the stress of the moment used the term "murder." Immediately afterward the thoughtless remark was regretted, but the damage had been done. The husband, deeply hurt, extended no hand in forgiveness; the wife stubbornly refused to ask it. Each was "too proud." To show humility, they thought, was the sign of a groveling spirit.

As in so many other instances where a mistake has been made, no distinction could be seen between the pride of dignity, of self-respect and the stubborn, unreasoning pride which blights our judgment and will not forgive or be forgiven. Many of us, perhaps, have preserved a silence for a few hours or even several days rather than "give in," forgetting that the breach is likely to become widened until finally it is beyond repair.

The tenderness of feeling that inspired this poem will be understood by anyone who has been estranged for any length of time from someone held dear.

Agree with thine adversary quickly
while thou art in the way with him,
for this is humility and humility is
peace.

THE CLOSED DOOR

I never crossed your threshold with a grief
   But that I went without it; never came
   Heart-hungry but you fed me, eased the blame
And gave the sorrow solace and relief.

I never left you but I took away
   The love that drew me to your side again
   Through that wide door that never could remain
Quite closed between us for a little day.

O friend, who gave and comforted, who knew
   So over well the want of heart and mind,
   Where may I turn for solace now, or find
Relief from this unceasing loss of you?

Be it for fault, for folly or for sin,
   Oh, terrible my penance and most sore—
   To face the tragedy of that closed door
Whereby I pass and may not enter in.

THEODOSIA GARRISON

ONE THING AT A TIME

Work while you work,
  Play while you play;
That is the way
  To be cheerful and gay.

All that you do,
  Do with your might;
Things done by halves
  Are never done right.

One thing each time,
  And that done well,
Is a very good rule,
  As many can tell.

Moments are useless
  Trifled away;
So work while you work,
  And play while you play.

M. A. STODART

HUNGERING HEARTS

Some hearts go hungering thro' the world
  And never find the love they seek.
Some lips with pride or scorn are curled
  To hide the pain they may not speak.
The eyes may flash, the mouth may smile—
And yet beneath them all the while
  The hungering heart is pining still.

For them does life's dull desert hold
  No fountain's shade, no gardens fair,
Nor gush of waters clear and cold,
  But sandy reaches wide and bare.
The foot may fail, the soul may faint,
  And weigh to earth the weary frame,
Yet still they make no weak complaint
  And speak no word of grief or blame.

O eager eyes, which gaze afar,
  O arms which clasp the empty air,
Not all unmarked your sorrows are,
  Not all unpitied your despair.
Smile, patient lips, so proudly dumb—
  HAVE FAITH! Before life's tent is furled
Your recompense shall come,
  O hearts that hunger through the world!

AUTHOR UNKNOWN

THE JOY OF INCOMPLETENESS

If all our life were one broad glare
  Of sunlight clear, unclouded:
If all our path were smooth and fair,
  By no soft gloom enshrouded;
If all life's flowers were fully blown
  Without the sweet unfolding,
And happiness were rudely thrown
  On hands too weak for holding—
Should we not miss the twilight hours,
  The gentle haze and sadness?
Should we not long for storms and showers
  To break the constant gladness?

If none were sick and none were sad,
  What service could we render?
I think if we were always glad
  We scarcely could be tender.
Did our beloved never need
  Our patient ministration,
Earth would grow cold and miss indeed
  Its sweetest consolation:
If sorrow never claimed our heart
  And every wish were granted
Patience would die, and hope depart—
  Life would be disenchanted.

ALBERT CROWELL

FIRM BELIEF

The thing that numbs the heart is this:
　　That men cannot devise
Some scheme of life to banish fear
　　That lurks in most men's eyes.

Fear of the lack of shelter, food,
　　And fire for winter's cold;
Fear of their children's lacking these,
　　This in a world so old.

This is my sure, my very firm belief:
That life, to one born whole, is worth the living,
Well worth the taking, having, and the giving.

AUTHOR UNKNOWN

BARTER

I will exchange a city for a sunset,
The tramp of legions for a wind's wild cry;
And all the braggart thrusts of steel triumphant
For one far summit, blue against the sky.

MARIE BLAKE

MIDWINTER

My window looks upon a world grown gray,
    Where grim trees seem like troubled men in prayer;
Smoke pours from chimneys, telling that the day
    Is drear—that piercing winds have chilled the air.

No songbird trills—only the sparrows wait
    Hunched in their feathers, for the proffered crumb;
It is as if some stern, relentless fate
    Had gripped the earth and left it tired and numb.

Even the far-off whistling of a train
    Sounds weary, dwindles to a ghostly wail;
Does all the world reflect war's gloomy strain,
    Wondering what foes, what evils may assail?

But spring will come—of this there is no doubt,
    With blossoming bough . . . if mankind would implore
The powers that be to put war's curse to rout,
    Could peace not bloom, too, in the world once more?

MARGARET E. BRUNER

*I lift up mine eyes unto the hills whence cometh my
strength.*

PSALMS

THE QUIET LIFE

Happy the man, whose wish and care
A few paternal acres bound,
Content to breathe his native air
      In his own ground.

Whose herds with milk, whose fields with bread,
Whose flocks supply him with attire;
Whose trees in summer yield him shade,
      In winter, fire.

Blest, who can unconcern'dly find
Hours, days, and years, slide soft away
In health of body, peace of mind,
      Quiet by day.

Sound sleep by night; study and ease
Together mix'd; sweet recreation,
And innocence, which most does please
      With meditation.

Thus let me live, unseen, unknown;
Thus unlamented let me die;
Steal from the world, and not a stone
      Tell where I lie.

                      ALEXANDER POPE

BEFORE IT IS TOO LATE

If you have a tender message,
  Or a loving word to say,
Do not wait till you forget it,
  But whisper it today;
The tender word unspoken,
  The letter never sent,
The long forgotten messages,
  The wealth of love unspent—
For these some hearts are breaking,
  For these some loved ones wait;
So show them that you care for them
  Before it is too late.

           FRANK HERBERT SWEET

Oh, face to face with trouble,
  Friend, I have often stood,
To learn that pain hath sweetness,
  To know that God is good.
Arise and meet the daylight,
  Be strong and do your best,
With an honest heart and a childlike trust
  That God will do the rest.

           MARGARET E. SANGSTER

I NEVER KNEW A NIGHT SO BLACK

I never knew a night so black
Light failed to follow on its track.
I never knew a storm so gray
It failed to have its clearing day.
I never knew such bleak despair
That there was not a rift, somewhere.
I never knew an hour so drear
Love could not fill it full of cheer!

JOHN KENDRICK BANGS

WORRIES

Take yesterday's worries and sort them all out
And you'll wonder whatever you worried about.
Look back, at the cares that once furrowed your brow,
I fancy you'll smile at most of them now.
They seemed terrible then, but they really were not,
For once out of the woods, all the fears are forgot.

AUTHOR UNKNOWN

TRUE HAPPINESS

These are the things which once possessed
Will make a life that's truly blessed:
A good estate on healthy soil,
Not got by vice, nor yet by toil;
Round a warm fire a pleasant joke,
With chimney ever free from smoke;
A strength entire, a sparkling bowl,
A quiet wife, a quiet soul,
A mind as well as body whole;
Prudent simplicity, constant friends,
A diet which no art commends;
A merry night without much drinking,
A happy thought without much thinking;
Each night by quiet sleep made short;
A will to be but what thou art:
Possessed of these all else defy,
And neither wish nor fear to die.

MORRIS TALPALAR

FRIENDSHIP

Dear friend, I pray thee, if thou wouldst be proving
   Thy strong regard for me,
Make me no vows. Lip service is not loving;
   Let thy faith speak for thee.

Swear not to me that nothing can divide us—
   So little such oaths mean.
But when distrust and envy creep beside us,
   Let them not come between.

Say not to me the depths of thy devotion
   Are deeper than the sea;
But watch, lest doubt or some unkind emotion
   Embitter them for thee.

Vow not to love me ever and forever,
   Words are such idle things;
But when we differ in opinions, never
   Hurt me by little stings.

I'm sick of words: they are so lightly spoken,
   And spoken, are but air.
I'd rather feel thy trust in me unbroken
   Than list thy words so fair.

If all the little proofs of trust are heeded,
   If thou art always kind,
No sacrifice, no promise will be needed
   To satisfy my mind.

                   ELLA WHEELER WILCOX

PRAYER FOR SHUT-INS

Because, dear Lord, their way is rough and steep,
And some are sore perplexed, and some do weep,
We come to ask that Thou wilt show the way
And give Thy rod and staff to be their stay.

Especially, dear Lord, for these we ask,
Who have not strength to meet their task;
And for all weary on the road
Please give fresh courage, ease their load.

                RUTH WINANT WHEELER

SALUTATION TO THE DAWN

Look to this day!
For it is life, the very life of life.
In its brief course
Lie all the verities and realities of your existence:

The bliss of growth;
The glory of action;
The splendor of achievement;
For yesterday is but a dream,
And tomorrow is only a vision;
But today, well lived, makes every yesterday a dream of
    happiness,
And every tomorrow a vision of hope.
Look well, therefore, to this day!

KALIDASA—TRANSLATED FROM THE SANSKRIT

THREE GATES OF GOLD

If you are tempted to reveal
    A tale to you someone has told
About another, make it pass,
    Before you speak, three gates of gold;
These narrow gates. First, "Is it true?"
    Then, "Is it needful?" In your mind
Give truthful answer. And the next
    Is last and narrowest, "Is it kind?"
And if to reach your lips at last
    It passes through these gateways three,
Then you may tell the tale, nor fear
    What the result of speech may be.

BETH DAY

UNSUBDUED

I have hoped, I have planned, I have striven,
  To the will I have added the deed;
The best that was in me I've given,
  I have prayed, but the gods would not heed.

I have dared and reached only disaster,
  I have battled and broken my lance;
I am bruised by a pitiless master
  That the weak and the timid call chance.

I am old, I am bent, I am cheated
  Of all that Youth urged me to win;
But name me not with the defeated,
  Tomorrow again, *I begin.*

S. E. KISER

THERE IS A LONELINESS

There is a loneliness on city streets
  More desolate than crag or wind-swept hill;
So near to others, still no welcome greets
  The ear with understanding and good will.

Sometimes I think that each one strives to hide,
　Masklike, the secret longings of the heart,
And yet, their stolid countenances confide
　A message that the lips dare not impart.

The brain grows dizzy while the eye looks on
　This pageant that forever marches by,
Till human folk seem but the cast-off spawn
　Of earth, with none to heed their inmost cry,
Ah then, do things inanimate, field and tree,
Seem clothed in friendship's calm security.

MARGARET E. BRUNER

LIFE

An infant—wailing in nameless fear;
　A shadow, perchance, in the quiet room,
Or the hum of an insect flying near,
　Or the screech owl's cry in the outer gloom.

A little child on the sun-checked floor;
　A broken toy, and a tear-stained face;
A young life clouded, a young heart sore,
　And the great clock, Time, ticks on apace.

A maiden weeping in bitter pain;
　Two white hands clasped on an aching brow;
A blighted faith, a fond hope slain,
　A shattered trust, and a broken vow.

A matron holding a baby's shoe;
  The hot tears gather and fall at will
On the knitted ribbon of white and blue,
  For the foot that wore it is cold and still.

An aged woman upon her bed,
  Worn and wearied, and poor and old,
Longing to rest with the happy dead;
  And thus the story of life is told.

Where is the season of careless glee;
  Where is the moment that holds no pain?
Life has its crosses from infancy
  Down to the grave—ARE ITS HOPES IN VAIN?

ELLA WHEELER WILCOX

WHATEVER IS—IS BEST

We know as we grow older
  And our eyes have clearer sight
That under each sad wrong, somewhere
  There lies the root of right!

We know that the soul is aided
  Sometimes by the heart's unrest
And to grow, means often to suffer
  That whatever is—is best.

We know there are few errors
　　In the great eternal plan,
And that all things work together
　　For the final good of man.

That each sorrow has its purpose
　　By the sorrowing, oft unguessed:
That as sure as the sun brings morning,
　　Whatever is—is best.

ELLA WHEELER WILCOX

The language of friendship is not words but meanings.
It is an intelligence above language.

THE BOOMERANG

One unkind word in the early morn
　　Will poison the thoughts for the day;
One unkind look to one we love
　　Will take all the sunshine away.
And twice all the sunshine we take away
From the lives of others at early day
We steal from ourselves the whole day long,
And we lose the beauty of earth's glad song.

One little smile when things go wrong
  Will drive off many a frown;
One pleasant look, though the thoughts do rage,
  Will put the tempter down.
And twice all the pleasure that we give out,
At the time when we are most tempted to pout,
Will sweeten our lives like a breath of May,
And the sun will shine through the whole glad day.

CARRIE MAY NICHOLS

MEDIATION No. 12672

MEDIATORS

General William J. Donovan—*Director, Office of Strategic Services, U. S. A.*
Dr. Paul Dawson Eddy—*President, Adelphi College, Garden City, N. Y.*
General John Reed Kilpatrick — *President, Madison Square Garden Corp.*

One problem that stands in the heart of every attempt to solve life's riddle is the mystery of pain. Every so often we hear of an apparently innocent person experiencing some great misfortune, and there comes to our lips the question—*Why?* Every story of seemingly undeserved heartache cries out for an explanation.

To those who have freshly experienced some disillusionment there is, perhaps, very little appeal in the philosophy so beautifully expressed by Emerson, that "our real blessings often appear to us in the shape of pains, losses and disappointments." He calls these blessings the rewards of suffering, the "compensations of calamity," but makes the reservation that we can only appreciate them after long intervals of time.

The reading of the poem *Compensation* was suggested by the presence of a certain woman of the tenements. She was old, and her active life was done. All her days she had wrestled with poverty in the slums of this great city. She had borne children, buried some of them, seen one or two go astray and others rise to positions of dignity and influence. She had nursed a husband through long years of pain and at last watched him fade into the shadow. What a life that woman had lived, and how deep its secrets were marked upon her face! But that face bore no sorrow, only wisdom and the great serenity of peace. She was like a great ship lying quietly at anchor in the evening glow. Battered and worn, no doubt! But she had breasted the waves of every sea and visited the ports of every clime. She had lived deeply and truly, had experienced life's dangers as well as its joys.

COMPENSATION

Who never wept knows laughter but a jest;
Who never failed, no victory has sought;
Who never suffered, never lived his best;
Who never doubted, never really thought;

Who never feared, real courage has not shown;
Who never faltered, lacks a real intent;
Whose soul was never troubled has not known
The sweetness and the peace of real content.

E. M. BRAINARD

They that sow in tears shall reap in joy.

WORK

How true it is when I am sad,
A little work can make me glad.
When frowning care comes to my door,
I work a while and fret no more.
I leave my couch harassed with pain,
I work, and soon I'm well again.
When sorrow comes and vain regret,
I go to work and soon forget.
Work soothes the soul when joys depart,
And often mends a broken heart.
The idle mind soon fills with murk,
So that's why God invented work.

J. W. THOMPSON

There are two births: The one when light
First strikes the new awakened sense;
The other when two souls unite,
And we must count our life from thence,
When you loved me and I loved you
Then both of us were born anew.

FROM "TO CHLOE" BY WILLIAM CARTWRIGHT

THE COMMON TASKS

The common tasks are beautiful if we
Have eyes to see their shining ministry.
The plowman with his share deep in the loam;
The carpenter whose skilled hands build a home;
The gardener working with reluctant sod,
Faithful to his partnership with God——
These are the artisans of life. And, oh,
A woman with her eyes and cheeks aglow,
Watching a kettle, tending a scarlet flame,
Guarding a little child—there is no name
For these great ministries, and eyes are dull
That do not see that they are beautiful;
That do not see within the common tasks
The simple answer to the thing God asks
Of any child, a pride within His breast;
That at our given work we do our best.

GRACE NOLL CROWELL

Sow a thought, you reap desire.
Sow a desire, you reap a habit.
Sow a habit, you reap a character.
Sow a character, you reap your destiny.

A VOW FOR NEW YEAR'S

Every hour and every minute
Has a New Year's Day tucked in it
And each single one of these
Is packed with possibilities—
Possibilities of pleasure,
Of sharing with some friend some treasure,
Of making a "Good morning" cheery—
Making a good one from a dreary—
Of shutting tight the lips to hide
A bit of gossip safe inside
Instead of letting it get out
To roam about and maybe do
More harm than you would like it to.
Let us take a little vow,
Since it is the New Year now,
To be more kind, more brave, more gay
This year and make each single day
That comes a model New Year's Day!

MARY CAROLYN DAVIES

MOTHER

Again your kindly, smiling face I see.
Do I but dream? And do my eyes deceive?
Again you whisper through the years to me,
I feel the pressure of your lips at eve.
I dream once more I sit upon your knee,
And hear sweet counsel that I should not grieve;
My hand in yours at twilight time as we
Talk low, and I your sweet caress receive.
At times I see your face with sorrow wrung,
Until, somewhat confused, I scarce believe
That I still dream. Your friends when you were young,
Your own great hopes, your cheer and laughter free
In some weird way are strangely haunting me.
O mother of my childhood's pleasant days!
Still whispering courage and dispelling fears
In daylight hours or quiet moonlight rays,
Are you a dream come from my younger years?
Or do you really walk along the ways,
And know my triumphs, or my inner tears,
That quickly cease when you close by me seem?
Let me sleep on, dear God, if I but dream.

MAX EHRMANN

REST

Are you very weary? Rest a little bit.
In some quiet corner, fold your hands and sit.
Do not let the trials that have grieved you all the day
Haunt this quiet corner; drive them all away!
Let your heart grow empty of every thought unkind
That peace may hover round you, and joy may fill your
    mind.
Count up all your blessings, I'm sure they are not few,
That the dear Lord daily just bestows on you.
Soon you'll feel so rested, glad you stopped a bit,
In this quiet corner, to fold your hands and sit.

                            AUTHOR UNKNOWN

BEATITUDES FOR A HOUSEWIFE

Blessed is she whose daily tasks are a labor of love; for her willing hands and happy heart translate duty into privilege, and her labor becomes a service to God and all mankind.

Blessed is she who opens the door to welcome both stranger and well-loved friend; for gracious hospitality is a test of brotherly love.

Blessed is she who mends stockings and toys and broken hearts; for her understanding is a balm to humanity.

Blessed is she who scours and scrubs; for well she knows that cleanliness is one expression of godliness.

Blessed is she whom children love; for the love of a child is more to be valued than fortune or fame.

Blessed is she who sings at her work; for music lightens the heaviest load and brightens the dullest chore.

Blessed is she who dusts away doubt and fear and sweeps out the cobwebs of confusion; for her faith will triumph over all adversity.

Blessed is she who serves laughter and smiles with every meal; for her buoyancy of spirit is an aid to mental and physical digestion.

Blessed is she who preserves the sanctity of the home; for hers is a sacred trust that crowns her with dignity.

MARY MAE OESCH

THE CELESTIAL SURGEON

If I have faltered more or less
In my great task of happiness;
If I have moved among my race
And shown no glorious morning face;
If beams from happy human eyes
Have moved me not; if morning skies,
Books, and my food, and summer rain
Knocked on my sullen heart in vain:—
Lord, thy most pointed pleasure take
And stab my spirit broad awake;
Or, Lord, if too obdurate I,
Choose thou, before that spirit die,
A piercing pain, a killing sin,
And to my dead heart run them in!

ROBERT LOUIS STEVENSON

THE LITTLE CHILD'S FAITH

It's a comfort to me in life's battle,
  When the conflict seems all going wrong,
When I seem to lose every ambition
  And the current of life grows too strong,

To think that the dusk ends the warfare,
   That the worry is done for the night;
And the little child there, at the window,
   Believes that his daddy's all right.

In the heat of the day and the hurry,
   I'm prompted so often to pause,
While my mind strays away from the striving,
   Away from the noise and applause.
The cheers may be meant for some other;
   Perhaps I have lost in the fight;
But the little child waits at the window,
   Believing his daddy's all right.

I can laugh at the downfalls and failure;
   I can smile in the trial and pain;
I can feel that in spite of the errors,
   The struggle has not been in vain.
If Fortune will only retain me
   That comfort and solace at night,
When the little child waits at the window,
   Believing his daddy's all right.

                              LOUIS EDWIN THAYER

*If a man is hurt in a street accident, an ambulance comes
quickly, but if he is broken in spirit, demoralized, afraid—
little is done—yet this person may be in far greater need of
the ambulance than the other.*

Flesh will heal and pain will fade
As nature and time repair,
But when the heart is bruised and torn
The scar—still lingers there.

CLAIRE RICHCREEK THOMAS

HEART WOUNDS

Cold steel may penetrate the flesh,
The wound may throb and smart,
But far more painful are the wounds
Inflicted on the heart.

Soothing balm may cease the pain
That body-blows impart
But what can heal the deep-cut wounds
Inflicted on the heart?

Yes—marks upon the flesh will fade,
Forgotten with the pain,
But when the heart is wounded thus,
The scar—will long remain.

CLAIRE RICHCREEK THOMAS

Take all sorrow out of life and you take away all richness, and depth, and tenderness. The capacity of sorrow belongs to our grandeur. It is the furnace that melts hearts together in love.

LIFE'S LESSON

There are times in one's life when all the world seems to turn against us. Our motives are misunderstood, our words misconstrued, an unkind word reveals to us the unfriendly feelings of others.

The fact is, that it is rare when injustice, or slights, patiently borne, do not leave the heart at the close of the day filled with a marvelous sense of peace—perhaps not at once —but after you've had a chance to reflect a bit. It is the seed God has sown, springing up and bearing fruit.

We learn, as the years roll onward and we leave the past behind, that much we had counted sorrow, but proved that God is kind; that many a flower we'd longed for had hidden a thorn of pain, and many a rugged by-path led to fields of ripened grain.

The clouds that cover the sunshine; they cannot banish the sun. And the earth shines out the brighter when the weary rain is done. We must stand in the deepest shadow to see the clearest light; and often through Wrong's own darkness comes the welcome strength of Right.

ELLA WHEELER WILCOX

There's a blessing on the hearth,
A special providence for fatherhood

ROBERT BROWNING

THE BRIDGE-BUILDER

An old man going a lone highway
Came at the evening, cold and gray,
To a chasm vast and wide and steep,
With waters rolling cold and deep.
The old man crossed in the twilight dim,
The sullen stream had no fears for him;
But he turned when safe on the other side,
And built a bridge to span the tide.

"Old man," said a fellow pilgrim near,
"You are wasting your strength with building here.
Your journey will end with the ending day,
You never again will pass this way.
You've crossed the chasm, deep and wide,
Why build you this bridge at eventide?"

The builder lifted his old gray head.
"Good friend, in the path I have come," he said,
"There followeth after me today
A youth whose feet must pass this way.
The chasm that was as nought to me
To that fair-haired youth may a pitfall be;
He, too, must cross in the twilight dim—
Good friend, I am building this bridge for him."

WILL ALLEN DROMGOOLE

IT CAN BE DONE

The man who misses all the fun
Is he who says, "It can't be done."
In solemn pride he stands aloof
And greets each venture with reproof.
Had he the power he'd efface
The history of the human race;
We'd have no radio or motor cars,
No streets lit by electric stars;
No telegraph nor telephone,
We'd linger in the age of stone.
The world would sleep if things were run
By men who say "It can't be done."

AUTHOR UNKNOWN

*Dedication to a purpose that never wavers—resolution—
this is the basic principle in the life of every truly great
character. He that resolves upon any great and good end
has, by that very resolution, clothed himself with power and
scaled the chief barrier to it.*

NEXT YEAR

"Next year, next year," we say,
   When come to nought
Our plans and projects gay,
   Our bright dreams, fraught

With brighter hopes, that shine
   On that far rim
Of life's horizon line,
   Where dreams lie dim

And touched with morning dew—
   "Next year, next year";
And while we plan anew
   The days grow sere.

The year flies by, and lo!
   We've left behind
The glory and the glow
   We hoped to find;

And raised again the clew
  We meant to heed—
The cherished plan to do
  Some cherished deed.

"Next year, next year!"
  Oh! why not now,
Delaying soul, this year
  Keep word and vow?

Oh! why not now and here,
  Why not today,
Before another year
  Shall run away?

Keep word and faith, or ere
  An hour's delay,
Make good the promise fair,
  TODAY, TODAY!

            NORA PERRY

A GENTLE WORD

A kindly word and a tender tone,—
To only God is their virtue known;
They can lift from the dust the abject head,
They can turn a foe to a friend instead;
The heart close-barred with passion and pride
Will fling at their knock its portal wide;

And the hate that blights, and the scorn that sears,
Will melt in the fountain of childlike tears.
What ice-bound barriers have been broken,
What rivers of love been stirred,
By a word in kindness spoken,
  By only a gentle word.

AUTHOR UNKNOWN

LITTLE THINGS

It's just the little homely things,
  The unobtrusive, friendly things,
The "won't-you-let-me-help-you" things
  That make our pathway light—
And it's just the jolly, joking things,
  The "never-mind-the-trouble" things,
The "laugh-with-me, it's funny" things
  That make the world seem bright.

For all the countless famous things,
  The wondrous, record-breaking things,
Those "never-can-be-equalled" things
  That all the papers cite,
Aren't like the little human things,
  The everyday-encountered things,
The "just-because-I-like-you" things
  That make us happy quite.

So here's to all the simple things,
   The dear "all-in-a-day's-work" things,
The "smile-and-face-your-troubles" things,
   Trust God to put them right!
The "done-and-then-forgotten" things,
   The "can't-you-see-I-love-you" things,
The hearty "I-am-with-you" things
   That make life worth the fight.

AUTHOR UNKNOWN

TOO LATE

What silences we keep, year after year
With those who are most near to us, and dear!
We live beside each other day by day,
And speak of myriad things, but seldom say
The full, sweet word that lies within our reach
Beneath the common ground of common speech.

Then out of sight and out of reach they go—
These close, familiar ones who loved us so;
And, sitting in the shadow they have left,
Alone with loneliness, and sore bereft,
We think with vain regret of some fond word
That once we might have said and they have heard.

This is the cruel cross of life—to be
Full visioned only when the ministry
Of death has been fulfilled, and in the place
Of some dear presence is but empty space.
What recollected services can then
Give consolation for the "might have been"?

NORA PERRY

COMMUNION

Quietly I enter the closet
Quietly I close the door.
Outside are the futilities,
The doubts and useless struggles;
Forgotten are the little things
That too long have shackled my mind
And held me prisoner.

Now unhurried and free
I contemplate God,
His mercy and His love.
Patiently I wait.

Lo, out of the shadows
Comes His presence.
Silently we visit.
From His wounded hand
I receive His balm
And His comfort.
I rest.

The door to the world is opened!
Eagerly I pass,
No longer futile,
Nor fearful,
Nor yet alone.
No longer I,
But, *We!*

P. M. SNIDER

BECAUSE YOU CARE

Because you care, each task will be much lighter,
    Each burden so much easier to bear;
And each new morning's outlook better, brighter,
    And each new day more blest, because you care.
Because you care, each joy will seem completer,
    Each treasure doubly dear and true and rare;
And in my heart I'll always find it sweeter
    To want the higher things, because you care.

FRANK CRANE

A rose to the living is more than
Sumptuous wreaths to the dead;
In filling love's infinite store
A rose to the living is more—

If graciously given before the
Hungering spirit is fled,
A rose to the living is more than
Sumptuous wreaths to the dead.

NIXON WATERMAN

RETALIATION

How often, for some trivial wrong,
In anger, we retaliate,
We learn, although it takes us long,
That life is far too brief for hate.

MARGARET E. BRUNER

CASUAL MEETING

We met upon a crowded street one day,
And for a fleeting space her glance held mine;
But we were strangers, there was nought to say,
So each passed on without a spoken sign.

Her eyes were deep and questioning, yet kind,
But were the eyes of one whose will was strong—
Of one who had a keen and eager mind,
And made of life a brave and buoyant song.

Strange, how this casual meeting stays with me,
 When things of far more magnitude have fled,
And yet the thought of it will always be
 Something to cherish, though no words were said.

MARGARET E. BRUNER

UNDERSTANDING

How blind men are! We surely cannot know
And judge the way men go!
Perhaps the grind of hectic years
Has won at last.

How sharp—how cruel can human judgments be!
The inmost heart of men we cannot see.
Thus has it been since time began;
Lay down the bruising stones we cast.

Of all the virtues which heaven has to give—
May it be with understanding that we live!

H. W. BLISS

WATCH YOURSELF GO BY

Just stand aside and watch yourself go by;
Think of yourself as "he" instead of "I."
Note closely as in other men you note
The bag-kneed trousers and the seedy coat.
Pick flaws; find fault; forget the man is you,
And strive to make your estimate ring true.
Confront yourself and look you in the eye—
Just stand aside and watch yourself go by.

Interpret all your motives just as though
You looked on one whose aims you did not know.
Let undisguised contempt surge through you when
You see you shirk, O commonest of men!
Despise your cowardice; condemn whate'er
You note of falseness in you anywhere.
Defend not one defect that shares your eye—
Just stand aside and watch yourself go by.

And then, with eyes unveiled to what you loathe,
To sins that with sweet charity you'd clothe,
Back to your self-walled tenement you'll go
With tolerance for all who dwell below.
The faults of others then will dwarf and shrink,
Love's chain grows stronger by one mighty link,
When you, with "he" as substitute for "I,"
Have stood aside and watched yourself go by.

STRICKLAND GILLILAN

THE GREATER GIFT

It was a dismal day when chilling rain
Like icy tears coursed down the window pane,
The clouds were dark and I was hedged about
With darker moods, but these were put to rout,
When to my ears there came a tapping sound,
So low at first as to be almost drowned
By other noises—then it grew more clear,
Until I knew some cherished friend was near;
And opening the door I heard your voice,
Soft-cadenced, kind, that made my heart rejoice;
You came to me because you sensed my need
Of comradeship, as if to intercede
With something of your spirit as a shield,
And yet you bore a gift—I saw revealed
A deeper motive . . . did you not foresee
That I had need of faith, serenity?
Two gifts you left, one was a healing token,
Yet of this greater gift no word was spoken.

MARGARET E. BRUNER

Think naught a trifle,
though it small appear;
Sands make the mountain,
Moments make the year,
and trifles—life.

ONLY A LITTLE THING

It was only a tiny seed,
　Carelessly brushed aside;
But it grew in time to a noxious weed,
　And spread its poison wide.

It was only a little leak,
　So small you might hardly see;
But the rising waters found the break,
　And wrecked the great levee.

It was only a single spark,
　Dropped by a passing train;
But the dead leaves caught, and swift and dark
　Was its work on wood and plain.

It was only a thoughtless word,
　Scarce meant to be unkind;
But it pierced as a dart to the heart that heard,
　And left its sting behind.

It may seem a trifle at most,
　The thing that we do or say;
And yet it may be that at fearful cost
　We may wish it undone someday.

M. P. HANDY

THE FIVE BEST DOCTORS

The five best doctors anywhere,
    And no one can deny it,
Are Doctors Sunshine, Water, Air,
    Exercise and Diet.

These five will gladly you attend,
    If only you are willing;
Your mind they'll cheer, your ills they'll mend,
    And charge you not one shilling.

                O. S. HOFFMAN

ONE OF US TWO

The day will dawn, when one of us shall harken
    In vain to hear a voice that has grown dumb,
And morns will fade, noons pale, and shadows darken,
    While sad eyes watch for feet that never come.

One of us two must sometime face existence
    Alone with memories that but sharpen pain.
And these sweet days shall shine back in the distance,
    Like dreams of summer dawns, in nights of rain.

One of us two, with tortured heart half broken,
　Shall read long-treasured letters through salt tears,
Shall kiss with anguished lips each cherished token,
　That speaks of these love-crowned, delicious years.

One of us two shall find all light, all beauty,
　All joy on earth, a tale forever done;
Shall know henceforth that life means only duty.
　Oh, God! Oh, God! have pity on that one.

ELLA WHEELER WILCOX

BEFORE AND AFTER MARRIAGE

We used to talk of so many things,
Roses and summer and golden rings,
Music and dances and books and plays,
Venice and moonlight and future days.

Now our chief subjects are food and bills,
Genevieve's measles and Johnny's ills;
New shoes for Betty, a hat for Jane,
Taxes, insurance, the mail and rain!

We used to say that Romance would stay.
We'd walk together a magic way!
Though we don't talk as in days of yore,
Strange, is it not, that I love you more?

ANNE CAMPBELL

MY NEIGHBOR'S ROSES

The roses red upon my neighbor's vine
Are owned by him, but they are also mine.
His was the cost, and his the labor, too,
But mine as well as his the joy, their loveliness to view.

They bloom for me and are for me as fair
As for the man who gives them all his care.
Thus I am rich because a good man grew
A rose-clad vine for all his neighbors' view.

I know from this that others plant for me,
And what they own my joy may also be;
So why be selfish when so much that's fine
Is grown for you upon your neighbor's vine?

A. L. GRUBER

And here is
MY NEIGHBOR'S REPLY

Your neighbor, sir, whose roses you admire,
Is glad indeed to know that they inspire
Within your breast a feeling quite as fine
As felt by him who owns and tends that vine.

That those fair flowers should give my neighbors joy
But swells my own, and draws therefrom alloy
Which would lessen its full worth, did I not know
That others' pleasure in the flowers grow.

Friend, from my neighbors and this vine I've learned
That sharing pleasure means a profit turned;
And he who shares the joy in what he's grown
Spreads joy abroad and doubles all his own.

AUTHOR UNKNOWN

BE HOPEFUL

Be hopeful, friend, when clouds are dark and days are
    gloomy, dreary,
Be hopeful even when the heart is sick and sad and weary.
Be hopeful when it seems your plans are all opposed and
    thwarted;
Go not upon life's battlefield despondent and fainthearted.
And, friends, be hopeful of yourself. Do bygone follies haunt
    you?
Forget them and begin afresh. And let no hindrance daunt
    you.
Though unimportant your career may seem as you begin it,
Press on, for victory's ahead. Be hopeful, friend, and win it.

STRICKLAND GILLILAN

A PRAYER FOR BROKEN LITTLE FAMILIES

God, pity broken little families
　Where there were four and now there are but three;
Where there were three and now there are but one or two;
　Pray, comfort these as Thou alone canst do.

Send peace to houses where there is a crib,
　Too wrinkleless its wild-rose-bordered spread,
Too smooth its pillow that, brief days ago,
　Hollowed to hold a tiny, curl-framed head;

Or where an untouched place is laid above
　An empty chair, facing which one must sit
And sup alone; or where a chintz-hung room
　No more has gay, untidy youth in it;

Or where a curtain now hangs straight that long
　Was knotted up so that a fragile hand
Might wave to neighbors as they came and went
　Past two tired eyes across the wintry land . . .

God, teach all broken little families
　To bear such losses self-conqueringly . . .
Understanding each other, day by day, more instinctively,
　Forbearing each other, day by day, more patiently,
Growing, day by day, more closely into oneness with each
　　other.

VIOLET ALLEYN STOREY

THE OLD WOMAN

As a white candle
In a holy place,
So is the beauty
Of an aged face.

As the spent radiance
Of the winter sun,
So is a woman
With her travail done.

Her brood gone from her,
And her thoughts as still
As the waters
Under a ruined mill.

JOSEPH CAMPBELL

DECISION

If love should count you worthy, and should deign
One day to seek your door and be your guest,
Pause! ere you draw the bolt and bid him rest,
If in your old content you would remain.
For not alone he enters; in his train
Are angels of the mists, the lonely quest,
Dreams of the unfulfilled and unpossessed,
And sorrow and life's immemorial pain.

He wakes desires you never may forget,
He shows you stars you never saw before,
He makes you share with him, for evermore,
The burden of the world's divine regret.
How wise you were to open not! and yet,
How poor if you should turn him from the door.

AUTHOR UNKNOWN

MINUTES OF GOLD

Two or three minutes—two or three hours,
What do they mean in this life of ours?
Not very much if but counted as time,
But minutes of gold and hours sublime,
If only we'll use them once in a while
To make someone happy—make someone smile.
A minute may dry a little lad's tears,
An hour sweep aside trouble of years.
Minutes of my time may bring to an end
Hopelessness somewhere, and bring me a friend.

AUTHOR UNKNOWN

PRAYER FOR A DAY'S WALK

God let me find the lonely ones
   Among the throng today
And let me say the word to take
   The loneliness away:
So many walk with aching hearts
   Along the old highway.

So many walk with breaking hearts,
   And no one understands;
They find the roadway rough and steep
   Across the barren lands;
God help me lighten weary eyes,
   And strengthen nerveless hands.

God help me brighten dreary eyes,
   And let my own grief be
A sure reminder of the grief
   Of those who walk with me.
When words fail—hands fail—let me go
   In silent sympathy.

                GRACE NOLL CROWELL

THE HEART'S ANCHOR

Think of me as your friend, I pray,
  And call me by a loving name;
I will not care what others say,
  If only you remain the same.
I will not care how dark the night;
  I will not care how wild the storm;
Your love will fill my heart with light
  And shield me close and keep me warm.

Think of me as your friend, I pray,
  For else my life is little worth:
So shall your memory light my way,
  Although we meet no more on earth.
For while I know your faith secure,
  I ask no happier fate to see:
Thus to be loved by one so pure
  Is honor rich enough for me.

WILLIAM WINTER

AWAY

I weary of these noisy nights,
  Of shallow jest and coarse "good cheer,"
Of jazzy sounds and brilliant lights.
  Come, Love, let us away from here.

Let us lay down this heavy load;
   And, side by side, far from the town,
Drive on some lovely country road;
   And, wondering, watch the sun go down.

What time is left to us, come, Love.
   The woods, the fields, shall make us whole;
The nightly pageantry above
   Our little world, keep sweet our soul.

No peace this city's madness yields—
   A tawdry world in cheap veneer.
Out there the lovely woods and fields.
   Come, Love, let us away from here.

MAX EHRMANN

YOU TELL ON YOURSELF

You tell what you are by the friends you seek,
By the very manner in which you speak,
By the way you employ your leisure time,
By the use you make of dollar and dime.

You tell what you are by the things you wear,
By the spirit in which you burdens bear,
By the kind of things at which you laugh,
By records you play on the phonograph.

You tell what you are by the way you walk,
By the things of which you delight to talk,
By the manner in which you bear defeat,
By so simple a thing as how you eat.

By the books you choose from the well-filled shelf;
In these ways, and more, you tell on yourself.

AUTHOR UNKNOWN

THE PREACHER'S MISTAKE

The parish priest
Of austerity,
Climbed up in a high church steeple
To be nearer God,
So that he might hand
His word down to His people.

When the sun was high,
When the sun was low,
The good man sat unheeding
Sublunary things.
From transcendency
Was he forever reading.
And now and again
When he heard the creak
Of the weather vane a-turning,

He closed his eyes
And said, "Of a truth
From God I now am learning."

And in sermon script
He daily wrote
What he thought was sent from heaven,
And he dropped this down
On his people's heads
Two times one day in seven.

In his age God said,
"Come down and die!"
And he cried out from the steeple,
"Where art thou, Lord?"
And the Lord replied,
"Down here among my people."

WILLIAM CROSWELL DOANE

THE GIFT

Once, long ago, a friend gave me a book
  Of poems—gems, the fruit of many minds;
I read them, thoughtless of the toil they took—
  The words moved softly as a stream that winds.

But now I know the lines I glibly read
Perhaps were born of pain—a broken heart;
Regret that followed with its stealthy tread—
The arrow of remorse with searching dart.

For wisdom comes with time's stern tutelage;
The years are keys, unlocking many a door;
And sometimes as I read mist blurs the page,
Here soul meets soul, a precious golden store.

MARGARET E. BRUNER

MEDIATION No. 1458

MEDIATORS

Hon. James A. Farley—*Civic Leader*
Dr. Ralph W. Sockman—*Pastor of Christ Church, New York*
Norman Thomas—*Educator; Author*

The poem on the preceding page, *The Gift,* impressed me as being exceptionally true. It brought to mind a very dramatic situation I encountered, the behind-the-scenes story of the simple little poem that follows this text, *Life.* The author must, of course, remain anonymous. Surely a glance at this modest verse would never lead one to imagine the ominous situation which inspired it.

It is a story dealing with a tender friendship that existed between two people for some time, only to cease abruptly. Several years before the young woman, a writer of poetry and contributor to many of the better-class magazines, was introduced to the man at a poetry group. He was a prosperous young business executive and unmarried. The two discovered that their tastes and ideals were in many ways identical, and a warm friendship developed. The man made it quite clear, however, that he would never be in a position to offer marriage. Among other reasons, there were the deep-rooted objections on the part of his family to racial and religious differences. The young woman was apparently reconciled to this condition and was happy in the knowledge that here was a relationship which brought fulfillment. The man kept the friendship a secret from his family. As so often happens in this kind of arrangement, however, where meetings are held in secret, there could be no happy or conventional ending. So far as the man was concerned, it was a pleasant relationship while it lasted, but it could not continue indefinitely. He gradually discontinued seeing the young woman, claiming to have visited her casually but a few times in the last three years. One day he received in the mail a letter to the effect that she had experienced some reverses and needed three hundred dollars immediately. Surprised and concerned over this development, he forwarded her a portion of this sum but made certain to use an unidentifiable and otherwise empty envelope.

In view of the friendship that had existed for a period of several years, the young woman, deeply resentful over the man's failure to accompany his remittance with at least a word of recognition, attempted to communicate with him at his place of business, causing him considerable embarrassment. Stung that a relationship that had once allegedly featured protestations of such undying affection could end in what she considered so shabby a manner, the young woman telephoned his home for the first time in the entire period of their friendship to inform him that if her need meant so little to him she would proceed to put the entire matter of their previous association before his family. It was the contention of the man that while he would not be averse to assisting her, he was not going to be intimidated or made the victim of blackmail. The friendship was over, and he did not feel he had incurred any obligation. He was taken aback by these strange new developments. On the other hand, the woman, having first resigned herself to the separation, was beside herself with mortification now that the quality of his friendship became apparent. From her point of view she had given him years of her life, and if it was his intention to thus scorn her, there was no alternative but to deal with him accordingly.

Such was the delicate situation I found existing when the matter was brought to my attention. While this is not a pretty story, it tends to demonstrate the unpredictable developments that can take place, even in the lives of ordinarily well-disposed people, when a question of delicate human emotions is involved. It served to show that the law of cause and effect is apparently relentless, whether we think in terms of science or of human relations. Invariably we have to pay for what we do, and if we want special concessions there is usually some toll exacted, whether we like it or not.

According to the board, while there may have been an obligation of some kind implicit in the man's participation in this friendship, whatever its nature, it was hardly one to be settled on the basis of dollars and cents. The method of reprisal undertaken by the woman was hardly to be commended. Since she was apparently in need of help, however, an agreement in writing was entered into, satisfactory to both parties, in which this help was to be given. The agreement would become void in the event of any untoward action on the part of the woman.

The following day I received a note from her: "I feel that I attended a funeral last evening—the funeral of all I held dear—the beautiful faith I had in a loved one." Attached was this little poem, bringing to an end a matter which, were it not for mediation, doubtless would have been the subject of long-drawn-out litigation and embarrassment, ruinous to both parties.

LIFE

I've seen the moonbeam's shining light;
I've watched the lamb clouds in the night,
As stars shone clear and bright.

I've heard the mighty ocean's roar,
Lashing the waves against the shore,
While stormy was the night.

I've seen the bitter, seen the sweet,
I've learned at last that it is meet,
To accept justly what is right.

AUTHOR UNKNOWN

OUR OWN

If I had known in the morning
How wearily all the day
    The words unkind
    Would trouble my mind
I said when you went away,
I had been more careful, darling,
    Nor given you needless pain;
But we vex our own
With look and tone
    We might never take back again.

For though in the quiet evening
You may give me the kiss of peace,
    Yet it might be
    That never for me
The pain of the heart should cease.
How many go forth in the morning
    That never come home at night,
And hearts have broken
For harsh words spoken
    That sorrow can ne'er set right.

We have careful thoughts for the stranger,
And smiles for the sometime guest,
    But oft for our own
    The bitter tone,
Though we love our own the best.

Oh, lips with the curve impatient,
  And brow with that look of scorn,
'Twere a cruel fate
Were the night too late
  To undo the work of the morn.

MARGARET E. SANGSTER

ALONE

There should be two words, dearest, one made up
  Of all glad sounds that ever breathed on earth;
Of all the ecstasies that fill joy's cup,
  Of love, and peace, and happiness, and mirth.

The other, like a weary, wailing sigh,
  Full of sad tones in longing, hungry strain,
Hopeless, despairing, just a baffled cry
  Of love and loneliness and blank, numb pain.

One I would love—the other I would fear,
  These two words, chosen with consummate art;
One meaning we're *alone* together, dear,
  The other meaning we're *alone*—apart.

CAROLYN WELLS

THEN LAUGH

Build for yourself a strong-box,
  Fashion each part with care;
When it's strong as your hand can make it,
  Put all your troubles there;
Hide there all thought of your failures
  And each bitter cup that you quaff;
Lock all your heartaches within it,
  Then sit on the lid and laugh.

Tell no one else its contents,
  Never its secrets share;
When you've dropped in your care and your worry
  Keep them forever there;
Hide them from sight so completely
  That the world will never dream half;
Fasten the strong-box securely—
  Then sit on the lid and laugh.

                          BERTHA ADAMS BACKUS

AT THE DOOR

Children are at the door.
Shall I let them in?
If I let them in, I can do no more the work I love;
If I bid them go, I then can work no more
For thinking that I should have let them in
And worked no more.

Duty is at the door.
Shall I let her in?
If I let her in, my life must change its course;
If I bid her go, my life will change itself
For thinking that I should have let her in
And followed her.

Love is at the door.
Shall I let him in?
If I let him in, my heart's content may cease;
If I bid him go, I may weep bitter tears
For thinking that I should have let him in to wound me
With an arrow from his sheath.

LILLIE FULLER MERRIAM

GOOD NIGHT! GOOD NIGHT!

Curse the tongue in my head,
   That a guest has gone away
And I have left unsaid
   Much that heart meant to say:
God bless your evening road
   And bless tomorrow then;
Lighten whatever load
   And bring you here again.
Time crowds upon us black,
   But your talk had a glow
That fought the darkness back,
   And I did not tell you so
Because my clumsy tongue
   Lacks grace to give good night.
That was a homely wrong
   But in my power to right.
There are wrongs enough and more,
   Almost past hope to mend.
But by Fire and Food and Door
   Let this one have an end!

JOHN HOLMES

HOME

Home!
My very heart's desire is safe
Within thy walls;
The voices of my loved ones, friends who come,
My treasured books that rest in niche serene,
All make more dear to me thy haven sweet.
Nor do my feet
Desire to wander out except that they
May have the glad return at eventide—
Dear Home.

Home!
My very heart's contentment lies
Within thy walls.
No worldly calls hath power to turn my eyes
In longing from thy quietness. Each morn
When I go forth upon the duties of the day
I wend my way
Content to know that eve will bring me
Safely to thy walls again.
Dear Home.

NELLIE WOMACK HINES

TO THE NEW OWNER

Here is the house, in readiness for you;
  Empty, as far as any eye can see,
But I must warn you that there lingers here
  Some ineradicable part of me.

My heart was keen to every grace of it,
  Prideful of seasoned strength in beam and rafter—
My house! to guard against unloveliness,
  To make of it a citadel of laughter.

May your own tenancy be bright as mine,
  Who crossed the threshold in strong tender arms,
Unknowing one small rooftree could afford,
  For two, such sanctuary from alarms.

So, if you hear a small, thin sound at dusk,
  A rustle as of someone on the stair,
Please do not stir—it will be likely I,
  Hoping to find a mislaid dream somewhere!

LUCILE HARGROVE REYNOLDS

GOD BLESS YOU

I seek in prayerful words, dear friend,
  My heart's true wish to send you,
That you may know that, far or near,
  My loving thoughts attend you.

I cannot find a truer word,
  Nor better to address you;
Nor song, nor poem have I heard
  Is sweeter than God bless you!

God bless you! So I've wished you all
  Of brightness life possesses;
For can there any joy at all
  Be yours unless God blesses?

God bless you! So I breathe a charm
  Lest grief's dark night oppress you,
For how can sorrow bring you harm
  If 'tis God's way to bless you?

And so, "through all thy days
  May shadows touch thee never—"
But this alone—God bless thee—
  Then art thou safe forever.

                              AUTHOR UNKNOWN

IS IT A DREAM?

Is it a dream, and nothing more—this faith
That nerves our brains to thought, our hands to work
For that great day when wars shall cease, and men
Shall live as brothers in a unity
Of love—live in a world made splendid?

Is it a dream—this faith of ours that pleads
And pulses in our hearts, and bids us look,
Through mists of tears and time, to that great day
When wars shall cease upon the earth, and men,
As brothers bound by love of man and God,
Shall build a world as gloriously fair
As sunset skies, or mountains when they catch
The farewell kiss of evening on their heights?

In our hearts this question, in our minds
The haunting echoes of the song of war;
When will the nations cure the itching palm?
Change curse of pride to love of peace?
How long before such peace can pass our lips,
Can claim our minds and drive out all distrust?
When shall our fingers dare to drop the sword,
While with unquestioning eyes we reach two hands
In open comradeship to all the world?

G. A. STUDDERT-KENNEDY

THE WHIRLPOOL

He was caught in the whirlpool of dismay
   By a thoughtless remark he had said;
He had injured a friend in a nonchalant way,
   And the love they had cherished lay dead.
To his mirror he went, in its glass to confide,
   And his face was both haggard and pale,
And he asked of the glass, "Should I swallow the pride
   That is pinning me down like a nail?
Should I go to my friend with remorse on my face,
   A remorse that I honestly feel?
Should I beg him this whirlpool of shame to erase,
   In a soul-stirring voice of appeal?"
"As your heart so dictates," said a voice from the glass,
   "I advise you to follow its path,
And remember 'twill pay you to keep off the grass,
   That is bordered with ill words and wrath."
So he went to his friend and he asked most sincere,
   To be taken again to his heart
And the whirlpool of friendship once more does endear
   Those friends who had drifted apart.

If there's someone you know, whom you treated that way,
   And your heart is both heavy and blue,
Seek and find him again without further delay,
   Don't wait until he comes to you.

You'll find that the whirlpool of Love will replace,
  Every misunderstanding and strife.
It will give you the courage to meet face to face,
  The changeable Whirlpool of Life.

AUTHOR UNKNOWN

THERE IS ALWAYS A PLACE FOR YOU

There is always a place for you at my table,
  You never need be invited.
I'll share every crust as long as I'm able,
  And know you will be delighted.
There is always a place for you by my fire,
  And though it may burn to embers,
If warmth and good cheer are your desire
  The friend of your heart remembers!
There is always a place for you by my side,
  And should the years tear us apart,
I will face lonely moments more satisfied
  With a place for you in my heart!

ANNE CAMPBELL

TIME'S HAND IS KIND

For those who place their blooms on new-made graves
   And feel that life holds nought but emptiness,
Know that time's hand in kindness ever saves
   The heart from too much sorrow and distress.

Yet all deep wounds heal slowly, it would seem,
   But gradually the yearning pain will cease. . . .
Thus will your grief become a hallowed dream
   And, in its stead, will come a strange new peace.

MARGARET E. BRUNER

THE BLIND MAN

I see a blind man every day
   Go bravely down the street;
He walks as if the path were clear
   Before his steady feet.
Save when he fumbles with his cane,
   I almost feel he sees
The passers-by who smile at him,
   The flowers and the trees.

He comes to corners where the crowd
    Of traffic swirls about,
But when he hesitates, some hand
    Will always help him out.
He crosses pavements fearlessly—
    It is as if he knows
That there are unknown, watchful friends
    Along the way he goes!

Sometimes we walk through unseen paths,
    Sometimes the road ahead
Is shrouded in the mists of fear;
    But we are being led
As surely as the blind man is. . . .
    And, if we seem to sway,
A hand will find us in the dark
    And guide us on our way.

                    MARGARET E. SANGSTER

TO GIVE ONE'S LIFE

To give one's life through eighty years is harder
    Than to give it in one moment gloriously;
To make each instant a brown willow basket
    Heaped with fresh flowers and ferns; to ever be

A cup of never-failing cool spring water
    To those who walk a dusty road alone;
To succor with life-giving bread, regardless,
    Those who expect a stone.

To give one's life, on weary days and hopeless;
  To give one's life, hour after hour, and be
Ready to give again, again, is harder
  Than to give it in a moment, gloriously.

MARY CAROLYN DAVIES

RESOLVE

To keep my health!
To do my work!
To live!
To see to it I grow and gain and give!
Never to look behind me for an hour!
To wait in weakness, and to walk in power;
But always fronting onward to the light,
Always and always facing toward the right.
Robbed, starved, defeated, fallen, wide astray—
On, with what strength I have!
Back to the way!

CHARLOTTE PERKINS STETSON GILMAN

CONFIDE IN A FRIEND

When you're tired and worn at the close of day
And things just don't seem to be going your way,
When even your patience has come to an end,
Try taking time out and confide in a friend.

Perhaps he too may have walked the same road
With a much troubled heart and burdensome load,
To find peace and comfort somewhere near the end,
When he stopped long enough to confide in a friend.

For then are most welcome a few words of cheer,
For someone who willingly lends you an ear.
No troubles exist that time cannot mend,
But to get quick relief, just confide in a friend.

AUTHOR UNKNOWN

A PRAYER FOR EVERY DAY

Make me too brave to lie or be unkind.
Make me too understanding, too, to mind
The little hurts companions give, and friends,
The careless hurts that no one quite intends.
Make me too thoughtful to hurt others so.
Help me to know
The inmost hearts of those for whom I care,
Their secret wishes, all the loads they bear,
That I may add my courage to their own.
May I make lonely folks feel less alone,
And happier ones a little happier yet.
May I forget
What ought to be forgotten; and recall,
Unfailing, all
That ought to be recalled, each kindly thing,
Forgetting what might sting.

To all upon my way,
Day after day,
Let me be joy, be hope! Let my life sing!

MARY CAROLYN DAVIES

ART THOU LONELY?

Art thou lonely, O my brother?
Share thy little with another!
Stretch a hand to one unfriended,
And thy loneliness is ended.

JOHN OXENHAM

WHAT IS GOOD?

"What is the real good?"
  I asked in musing mood.
Order, said the law court;
  Knowledge, said the school;
Truth, said the wise man;
  Pleasure, said the fool;
Love, said the maiden;
  Beauty, said the page;
Freedom, said the dreamer;
  Home, said the sage;

Fame, said the soldier;
 Equity, said the seer;
Spoke my heart full sadly,
 "The answer is not here."
Then within my bosom
 Softly this I heard:
"Each heart holds the secret;
 Kindness is the word."

JOHN BOYLE O'REILLY

DEFINITION

I search among the plain and lovely words
To find what the one word "Mother" means. As well
Try to define the tangled song of birds,
The echo in the hills of one clear bell—
One cannot snare the wind—or catch the wings
Of shadows flying low across the wheat.
Ah—who can prison simple, natural things
That make the long days beautiful and sweet?

"Mother"—a word that holds the tender spell
Of all the dear, essential things of earth:
A home, clean sunlit rooms, and the good smell
Of bread, a table spread, a glowing hearth,
And love beyond the dream of anyone—
I search for words for her—and there are none.

GRACE NOLL CROWELL

THE SINCERE MAN

What gifts of speech a man may own,
　　What grace of manners may appear,
Have little worth unless his heart
　　Be honest, forthright and sincere.

The sincere man is like a rock,
　　As true as time; with honest eye
He looks you squarely in the face
　　Nor turns aside to make reply.

Nothing is hidden; there is no sham,
　　No camouflage to caution care,
No *ifs* or *buts* to haunt the mind,
　　Or secret doubts to linger there.

A crystal candor marks his speech,
　　With conscience clear he goes his way,
He does the thing he thinks is right
　　Nor cares a whit what others say.

Give me a man that is sincere,
　　And though a wealth of faults attend,
I shall clasp his hand in mine
　　And claim him as a trusted friend!

ALFRED GRANT WALTON

IF YOU HAD A FRIEND

If you had a friend strong, simple, true,
Who knew your faults and who understood;
Who believed in the very best of you,
And who cared for you as a father would;

If you had a friend like this, I say,
So sweet and tender, so strong and true
You'd try to please him in every way
And live at your bravest, now wouldn't you?

His worth would shine in the words you praised
You'd shout his praises—yet—now how odd?
You tell me you haven't got such a friend
You haven't?—I wonder—*What of God?*

ROBERT LEWIS

ETERNAL VALUES

Whatever else be lost among the years,
God still abides, and love remains the same.
And bravery will glimmer through men's tears,
And truth will keep its clean and upright name.
As long as life lasts there will ever be
Kindness and justice and high loyalty.

In a bewildered world these things will hold
The human heart from darkness and despair.
Old as the sun and moon and stars are old,
Remaining constant, they are ever there,
Lodestars for men to steer their courses by.
The eternal things of life can never die.

GRACE NOLL CROWELL

REMEMBRANCE

This memory of my mother stays with me
   Throughout the years: the way she used to stand
   Framed in the door when any of her band
Of children left . . . as long as she could see
Their forms, she gazed, as if she seemed to be
   Trying to guard—to meet some far demand;
   And then before she turned to tasks at hand,
She breathed a little prayer inaudibly.

And now, I think, in some far heavenly place,
   She watches still, and yet is not distressed,
But rather as one who, after life's long race,
   Has found contentment in a well-earned rest,
There, in a peaceful dreamlike reverie,
She waits, from earthly cares forever free.

MARGARET E. BRUNER

THE VOICE OF GOD

I sought to hear the voice of God,
    And climbed the topmost steeple.
But God declared: "Go down again,
    I dwell among the people."

                    LOUIS I. NEWMAN

Earth has no sorrow that heaven cannot heal.

GOOD-BYE

Good-bye, proud world! I'm going home:
Thou art not my friend, and I'm not thine.
Long through thy weary crowds I roam;
A river-ark on the ocean brine,
Long I've been tossed like the driven foam;
But now, proud world! I'm going home.

Good-bye to Flattery's fawning face;
To Grandeur with his wise grimace;
To upstart Wealth's averted eye;
To supple Office, low and high;

To crowded halls, to court and street;
To frozen hearts and hasting feet;
To those who go, and those who come;
Good-bye, proud world! I'm going home.

I am going to my own hearth-stone,
Bosomed in yon green hills alone—
A secret nook in a pleasant land,
Whose groves the frolic fairies planned;
Where arches green, the livelong day,
Echo the blackbird's roundelay,
And vulgar feet have never trod
A spot that is sacred to thought and God.

O, when I am safe in my sylvan home,
I tread on the pride of Greece and Rome;
And when I am stretched beneath the pines,
Where the evening star so holy shines,
I laugh at the lore and the pride of man,
At the sophist schools and the learned clan;
For what are they all, in their high conceit,
When man in the bush with God may meet?

RALPH WALDO EMERSON

There is so much of loneliness
    On this uncharted earth
It seems each one's a prisoner
    Within a cell from birth.

There is such need for union,
 Such need for clasping hands,
Yet we deny the brotherhood
 The human heart demands.

AUTHOR UNKNOWN

"NO!"

Learn to speak this little word
In its proper place—
Let no timid doubt be heard,
Clothed with sceptic grace;
Let thy lips, without disguise,
Boldly pour it out;
Though a thousand dulcet lies
Keep hovering about.
For be sure our lives would lose
Future years of woe;
If our courage could refuse
The present hour with "No."

ELIZA COOK

RETRIBUTION

The mills of the gods grind late, but they grind fine.

GREEK POET

Though the mills of God grind slowly, yet they grind
    exceeding small;
Though with patience He stands waiting, with exactness
    grinds He all.

FROM "RETRIBUTION"
BY HENRY WADSWORTH LONGFELLOW

THE LONELY DOG

He often came and stood outside my door
    And gazed at me with puzzled, wondering eyes,
    Like those of humankind by grief made wise—
Who feel that life has little left in store.
And yet, he never looked unkempt and poor
    As if he deemed a meaty bone a prize;
    Instead, it seemed he wore a human guise
As though the heart of man he would explore.

Then one night on the street he followed me
    Persistently, until I turned and said
Sharp, angry words, which made him quickly flee—
    His spirit wounded and uncomforted,
And now at last I think I comprehend:
He only craved an understanding friend.

                                MARGARET E. BRUNER

BEYOND THE GRAVE

How often have we known a dog to be
    More loyal than the race of humankind . . .
Although it seems a dog can somehow see
    The very inmost caverns of the mind.

And yet he never looks upon a friend
    With scorn, even though the world that friend despise;
And when death claims his master—brings an end
    To comradeship—he grieves . . . his sorrowing eyes

Seem questioning, and yet to understand
    That this is something that must come to all,
But human folk can turn to tasks at hand
    To break the tension of its gloomy thrall.

It may be that the selfsame power that gave
    The dog his faithful, understanding heart
Will grant him life again beyond the grave,
    To meet with friends—where death can play no part.

                                MARGARET E. BRUNER

326

HOSPITAL

Here is the haven: pain touched with soft magic:
    Errands all of mercy. Here the sweet
Ministry of white hands to meet the tragic
    Miracle of death, the brave defeat.

Here is the harbor, builded for the broken,
    Echoing halls where gentleness has trod.
Here our eyes are blinded by a token . . .
    A shaft of glory from the throne of God.

WILFRED FUNK

SO LIVE

So live that when thy summons comes to join
The innumerable caravan, which moves
To that mysterious realm, where each shall take
His chamber in the silent halls of death,
Thou go not like the quarry slave at night,
Scourged to his dungeon, but, sustained and soothed
By an unfaltering trust, approach thy grave
Like one who wraps the drapery of his couch
About him, and lies down to pleasant dreams.

FROM "THANATOPSIS" BY WILLIAM CULLEN BRYANT

327

LIFE OWES ME NOTHING

Life owes me nothing. Let the years
Bring clouds or azure, joy or tears;
  Already a full cup I've quaffed;
  Already wept and loved and laughed,
And seen, in ever-endless ways,
New beauties overwhelm the days.

Life owes me nought. No pain that waits
Can steal the wealth from memory's gates;
  No aftermath of anguish slow
  Can quench the soul fire's early glow.
I breathe, exulting, each new breath,
Embracing Life, ignoring Death.

Life owes me nothing. One clear morn
Is boon enough for being born;
  And be it ninety years or ten,
  No need for me to question when.
While Life is mine, I'll find it good,
And greet each hour with gratitude.

AUTHOR UNKNOWN

MOTHER

For such as you, I do believe,
Spirits their softest carpets weave,
And spread them out with gracious hand
Wherever you walk, wherever you stand.

For such as you, of scent and dew
Spirits their rarest nectar brew,
And where you sit and where you sup
Pour beauty's elixir in your cup.

For all day long, like other folk,
You bear the burden, wear the yoke,
And yet when I look into your eyes at eve
You are lovelier than ever, I do believe.

HERMAN HAGEDORN

A THANKFUL HEART

Lord, Thou hast given me a cell
    Wherein to dwell,
A little house whose humble roof
    Is weatherproof. . . .
Low is my porch as is my fate,
    Both void of state,

And yet the threshold of my door
   Is worn by the poor
Who hither come and freely get
   Good words or meat.
'Tis Thou that crown'st my glittering hearth
   With guileless mirth.
All these and better Thou dost send
   Me to this end,
That I should render for my part
   A thankful heart.

ROBERT HERRICK

LOVE'S PHILOSOPHY

The fountains mingle with the river,
   And the rivers with the ocean,
The winds of heaven mix forever
   With a sweet emotion;
Nothing in the world is single;
   All things by a law divine
In one another's being mingle—
   Why not I with thine?

See the mountains kiss high heaven,
   And the waves clasp one another;
No sister flower would be forgiven
   If it disdain'd its brother:

And the sunlight clasps the earth,
   And the moonbeams kiss the sea;—
What are all these kissings worth,
   If thou kiss not me?

PERCY BYSSHE SHELLEY

PLEA FOR TOLERANCE

If we but knew what forces helped to mold
   The lives of others from their earliest years—
   Knew something of their background, joys and tears,
And whether or not their youth was drear and cold,
Or if some dark belief had taken hold
   And kept them shackled, torn with doubts and fears
   So long it crushed the force that perseveres
And made their hearts grow prematurely old,—

Then we might judge with wiser, kindlier sight,
   And learn to put aside our pride and scorn . . .
Perhaps no one can ever quite undo
   His faults or wholly banish some past blight—
The tolerant mind is purified, reborn,
   And lifted upward to a saner view.

MARGARET E. BRUNER

THE ARROW AND THE SONG

I shot an arrow into the air,
It fell to earth, I knew not where;
For so swiftly it flew, the sight
Could not follow it in its flight.

I breathed a song into the air,
It fell to earth, I knew not where;
For, who has sight so keen and strong
That it can follow the flight of song?

Long, long afterward, in an oak
I found the arrow, still unbroke;
And the song, from beginning to end,
I found again in the heart of a friend.

HENRY WADSWORTH LONGFELLOW

WORRY

Worry—is like a distant hill
 We glimpse against the sky.
We wonder how we ever will
 Get up a hill so high.

Yet, when we reach the top, we see
   The roadway left behind
Is not as steep and sheer as we
   Have pictured in our mind.

AUTHOR UNKNOWN

TODAY

I have spread wet linen
On lavender bushes,
I have swept rose petals
From a garden walk.
I have labeled jars of raspberry jam,
I have baked a sunshine cake;
I have embroidered a yellow duck
On a small blue frock.
I have polished andirons,
Dusted the highboy,
Cut sweet peas for a black bowl,
Wound the tall clock,
Pleated a lace ruffle . . .
To-day
I have lived a poem.

ETHEL ROMIG FULLER

GOD'S WAYS ARE STRANGE

God's ways are strange; He chastens those
He loves and gives them more of pain
Than joy—and bids their hearts refrain
From hatred of their darkest foes.

Yet we of earth would not impose
On those we love a galling chain—
God's ways are strange.

And I have wondered that He chose
Such trying means with which to gain
A lasting good; but why complain
Of thorns? Enough to have the rose—
God's ways are strange.

MARGARET E. BRUNER

CLOAK OF LAUGHTER

I wear a cloak of laughter
  Lest anyone should see
My dress of sorrow underneath
  And stop to pity me.

I wear a cloak of laughter
  Lest anyone should guess
That what is hid beneath it
  Is less than happiness. . . .

But, ah, what does it matter
  To you who are so wise?
My cloak falls tattered at my feet
  Before your tender eyes.

For cloaks to cover sorrow
  Are meant for stranger folk;
One cannot hide away from friends
  Beneath a laughing cloak.

Oh, futile cloak of laughter,
  How frail you are and thin!
Love looks through you so easily
  And sees the grief within.

                    ABIGAIL CRESSON

"The gem cannot be polished without friction, nor man perfected without trials."

CONFUCIUS

IF LINCOLN SHOULD RETURN

If Lincoln were to come again to earth,
   And view this land of plenty and yet know
That countless of its people knew but dearth,
   And in their hearts was bitterness and woe,
Those sorrowing eyes of his perhaps would wear
   An even more profound and troubled gaze,
And though he faltered he would not despair,
   But find new lamps to light the darkened ways.

For only he who once walked hand in hand
   With poverty can feel for those whose lot
It is to wear the stigma of the brand
   Of alms and doles that leaves an ugly blot—
The heart that bled for everyone who knew
Distress would somehow know the thing to do.

                       MARGARET E. BRUNER

WHAT THE KING HAS

What the king has
   That have I:
Rose-gold of dawn,
   Bejeweled sky,
A wealth of days
   Slipping by.

What the king has
   That have I!
Hopes deferred,
   Ambitions high,
Hungerings to satisfy.

What the king has
   That have I:
A crown of love
   Naught can buy,
Once to live,
   Once to die.

ETHEL ROMIG FULLER

HUSBAND AND WIFE

Whatever I said and whatever you said,
         I love you.
The word and the moment forever have fled;
         I love you.
The breezes may ruffle the stream in its flow,
But tranquil and clear are the waters below;
And under all tumult you feel and you know
         I love you.

Whatever you did and whatever I did,
         I love you.
Whatever is open, whatever is hid,
         I love you.

337

The strength of the oak makes the tempest a mock,
The anchor holds firm in the hurricane's shock;
Our love is the anchor, the oak and the rock.
      I love you.

Whatever I thought and whatever you thought,
      I love you.
The mood and the passion that made it are naught;
      I love you.
For words, thoughts and deeds, though they rankle and
    smart,
May never delude us or hold us apart
Who treasure this talisman deep in the heart,
      "I love you."

ARTHUR GUITERMAN

A FRIEND

      'Tis a little thing
To give a cup of water; yet its draught
Of cool refreshment, drained by fevered lips,
May give a shock of pleasure to the frame
More exquisite than when nectarean juice
Renews the life of joy in happier hours.
It is a little thing to speak a phrase
Of common comfort which by daily use
Has almost lost its sense, yet on the ear
Of him who thought to die unmourned 'twill fall
Like choicest music, fill the glazing eye

338

With gentle tears, relax the knotted hand
To know the bonds of fellowship again;
And shed on some unhappy soul
A sense, to him who else were lonely,
That a friend is near and feels.

SIR THOMAS N. TALFOURD

Love much. Earth has enough of bitter in it;
　Cast sweets into its cup whene'er you can.
No heart so hard but love at last may win it.
　Yes, love on through doubt and darkness, and believe
There is no thing which love may not achieve.

ELLA WHEELER WILCOX

WHAT'S IN IT FOR ME?

We fancied he'd share in our cause. Instead,
"There is nothing in it for me!" he said.
He passed up pity and play and mirth
And counted his time to the penny's worth.
Ask for his help, and this would be
His answer: "What is there in it for me?"

Nothing it meant if you said: "In this
Perhaps is friendship you'll some day miss.
Here is a task that won't pay in gold,
But will leave you prouder when you grow old.

Though nothing for this will your purse collect,
It will pay you richly in self-respect."

"What is there in it for me?" he said.
We mentioned pride, but he shook his head.
"The joy of giving," he flicked his hand—
That he never could understand.
And he found when life's last far bend was turned
That money was all he had ever earned.

EDGAR A. GUEST

TAKE TIME TO LIVE

Take time to live;
The world has much to give,
Of faith and hope and love:
Of faith that life is good,
That human brotherhood
Shall no illusion prove;
Of hope that future years
Shall bring the best, in spite
Of those whose darkened sight
Would stir our doubts and fears;
Of love, that makes of life,
With all its griefs, a song;
A friend, of conquered wrong;
A symphony, of strife.
Take time to live,
Nor to vain mammon give
Your fruitful years.

Take time to live;
The world has much to give
Of sweet content; of joy
At duty bravely done;
Of hope, that every sun
Shall bring more fair employ.
Take time to live,
For life has much to give
Despite the cynic's sneer
That all's forever wrong;
There's much that calls for song.
To fate lend not your ear.
Take time to live;
The world has much to give.

THOMAS CURTIS CLARK

FOR A NEW HOME

Oh, love this house, and make of it a Home—
A cherished, hallowed place.
Root roses at its base, and freely paint
The glow of welcome on its smiling face!
For after friends are gone, and children marry,
And you are left alone . . .
The house you loved will clasp you to its heart,
Within its arms of lumber and of stone.

ROSA ZAGNONI MARINONI

THE HUMAN HEART

There's a heap o' love in the human heart
　　If we just dig down a bit;
It's the masterpiece of the Mighty Hand
　　And He gave His best to it.
There's a heap o' good in the most of men,
　　Just underneath the skin,
And much would show that we never know,
　　Could we only look within.

There's a lot inside that we never see,
　　And perhaps we never know,
'Til fortunes turn and we're down and out,
　　Or sickness strikes us low.
But the heart is right in the most of men,
　　When the truth is really known,
And we often find that the heart is kind
　　That we thought was cold as stone.

We sometimes tire of the road so rough
　　And the hill that seems so steep,
And we sometimes feel that hope is gone,
　　As we sit alone and weep;
And then when our faith is burning low
　　And we lose our trust in men,
True friends appear with a word of cheer
　　And the sun comes out again.

And so I claim that the heart of man
  Is about what it ought to be,
For it's made of goodness through and through,
  Could we look inside and see.
God made all things and He made them well,
  On the true and perfect plan,
But He did His best in the greatest test
  When He made the heart of man.

FRANK CARLETON NELSON

PATTY-POEM

She never puts her toys away;
Just leaves them scattered where they lay—
I try to scold her, and I say
"You make me mad!"

But when to bed she has to chase,
The toys she left about the place
Remind me of her shining face,
And make me glad.

When she grows up and gathers poise
I'll miss her harum-scarum noise,
And look in vain for scattered toys—
And I'll be sad.

NICK KENNY

THANKS BE TO GOD

I do not thank Thee, Lord,
That I have bread to eat while others starve;
Nor yet for work to do
While empty hands solicit Heaven;
Nor for a body strong
While other bodies flatten beds of pain.
No, not for these do I give thanks!

But I am grateful, Lord,
Because my meager loaf I may divide;
For that my busy hands
May move to meet another's need;
Because my doubled strength
I may expend to steady one who faints.
Yes, for all these do I give thanks!

For heart to share, desire to bear
And will to lift,
Flamed into one by deathless Love—
Thanks be to God for this!
Unspeakable! His Gift!

JANIE ALFORD

RECIPE FOR LIVING

Some things a man must surely know,
   If he is going to live and grow:
He needs to know that life is more
   Than what a man lays by in store,
That more than all he may obtain,
   Contentment offers greater gain.
He needs to feel the thrill of mirth,
   To sense the beauty of the earth,
To know the joy that kindness brings
   And all the worth of little things.
He needs to have an open mind,
   A friendly heart for all mankind,
A trust in self—without conceit—
   And strength to rise above defeat.
He needs to have the will to share,
   A mind to dream, a soul to dare,
A purpose firm, a path to plod,
   A faith in man, a trust in God.

              ALFRED GRANT WALTON

I AM YOUR WIFE

Oh, let me lay my head tonight upon your breast
And close my eyes against the light. I fain would rest.
I'm weary and the world looks sad. This worldly strife
Turns me to you! And, oh, I'm glad to be your wife.
Though friends may fail or turn aside, yet I have you.
And in your love I may abide for you are true.
My only solace in each grief, and in despair
Your tenderness is my relief. It soothes each care.
If joys of life could alienate this poor weak heart
From yours, then may no pleasure great enough to part
Our sympathies fall to my lot. I'd ever remain
Bereft of friends, though true or not, just to retain
Your true regard, your presence bright, thru care and strife;
And, oh, I thank my God tonight *I am your wife.*

AUTHOR UNKNOWN

LOVE IS KIND

Each man is limited by inborn traits;
　　Beyond a certain point he cannot go;
The wise excel in high or low estates;
　　The good mock not good workers just below.

If one can lift a weight of half a ton,
　Give him full credit, yet not praise him more
Than one who, lifting less, his best has done,
　Nor give the latter less than actual score.

We grant that each has striven toward the best,
　Yet judge by failure, not by worth or toil.
The "highest" is not worthier than the rest,
　And none should other's worthy effort spoil.

BENJAMIN KEECH

CONTENT

Content, content! within a quiet room
All warm and lit we meet; the outward gloom
Is like a folding arm about us pressed;
A space to love in, and a space to pray
We find; content, content!

DORA GREENWELL

THESE ARE NOT LOST

The look of sympathy, the gentle word,
Spoken so low that only angels heard;
The secret act of pure self-sacrifice,
Unseen by men, but marked by angels' eyes—
　These are not lost. . . .

The kindly plan devised for others' good,
So seldom guessed, so little understood,
The quiet, steadfast love that strove to win
Some wanderer from the ways of sin—
   These are not lost.

Not lost, O Lord! for in Thy city bright
Our eyes shall see the past by clearer light,
And things long hidden from our gaze below
Thou wilt reveal; and we shall surely know
   These are not lost.

RICHARD METCALF

Is there any worse fate that can befall a man in this world,
Than to live and grow old alone, unloving and unloved?

NEED OF LOVING

Folk need a lot of loving in the morning;
   The day is all before, with cares beset—
The cares we know, and they that give no warning;
   For love is God's own antidote for fret.

Folk need a heap of loving at the noontime—
   In the battle lull, the moment snatched from strife—
Halfway between the waking and the croon time,
   While bickering and worriment are rife.

Folk hunger so for loving at the nighttime,
  When wearily they take them home to rest—
At slumber song and turning-out-the-light time—
  Of all the times for loving, that's the best.

Folk want a lot of loving every minute—
  The sympathy of others and their smile!
Till life's end, from the moment they begin it,
  Folks need a lot of loving all the while.

STRICKLAND GILLILAN

I WOULD BE TRUE

I would be true, for there are those who trust me;
I would be pure, for there are those who care;
I would be strong, for there is much to suffer;
I would be brave, for there is much to dare.
I would be friend of all—the foe, the friendless;
I would be giving, and forget the gift,
I would be humble, for I know my weakness,
I would look up, and love, and laugh and lift.

HOWARD ARNOLD WALTER

WHY DO I LIVE?

I live for those who love me,
  For those who know me true,
For the heaven that bends above me,
  And the good that I can do;
For the wrongs that need resistance,
For the cause that lacks assistance,
For the future in the distance,
  And the good that I can do.

THOMAS GUTHRIE

LET'S FORGET

Let's forget the many troubles
  That the year now gone has brought;
Let's forget its pain and sorrow;
  Let's forget our burdened lot;
Let new hope and courage cheer us;
  Sunshine always follows rain;
There's a challenge in the Future;
  Men are needed now, again!

Let's forget deflated values;
   Money is no gauge of souls;
Let's forget restricted markets;
   Profit lies in higher goals;
Serve in love some weaker brother;
   There's so many need your smile;
Make the whole year bright for others,
   Then your life will be worth while.

Let's forget distrust and hatred;
   War from fear is oft aborning;
Let's forget our narrow boundings;
   Work for peace and greet its dawning;
Let's forget the self that's held us
   In our petty, cabined state;
Let us meet our challenge boldly
   And in meeting it be great.

CHARLES L. H. WAGNER

FOR THOSE WHO FAIL

"All honor to him, who shall win the fight,"
The world has cried for a thousand years,
But to him who tries and who fails and dies,
I give great honor and glory and tears;
Give glory and honor and pitiful tears
To all who fail in their deeds sublime;
Their ghosts are many in the van of years,
They were born with time in advance of time.

351

Oh! great is the hero who wins a name,
But greater many and many a time
Some pale-faced fellow who dies in shame
And lets God publish the thought sublime,
And great is the man with the sword undrawn,
And good is the man who refrains from wine,
But the man who fails and yet still fights on,
Lo, he is a twin brother of mine.

                              JOAQUIN MILLER

Before God's footstool to confess
A poor soul knelt, and bowed his head;
"I failed," he cried. The Master said,
"Thou didst thy best—that is success!"

"It is in loving, not in being loved,
    the heart finds its quest;
It is in giving, not in getting,
    our lives are blest."

FOR LOVE'S SAKE ONLY

If thou must love me, let it be for nought
Except for love's sake only. Do not say
"I love her for her smile—her look—her way
Of speaking gently,—for a trick of thought

That falls in well with mine, and certes brought
A sense of pleasant ease on such a day"—
For these things in themselves, Beloved, may
Be changed, or change for thee,—and love, so wrought,
May be unwrought so. Neither love me for
Thine own dear pity's wiping my cheeks dry,—
A creature might forget to weep, who bore
Thy comfort long, and lose thy love thereby!
But love me for love's sake, that evermore
Thou mayst love on, through love's eternity.

ELIZABETH BARRETT BROWNING

REBIRTH

Sometimes we go our way carefree;
   No trouble comes to mar
The routine of our lives, and we
   Forget there is a scar
Or wound in other lives, till pain
   Descends on someone near
To us, and then our hearts regain
   Lost kindliness; we hear
With understanding of the woes
   Of others—a rebirth
Comes, and we feel for all of those
   Who suffer here on earth.

MARGARET E. BRUNER

JUST TO BE NEEDED

"She always seems so tied" is what friends say;
She never has a chance to get away.
Home, husband, children, duties great or small,
Keep her forever at their beck and call.
But she confides, with laughter in her eyes,
She never yet felt fretted by these ties.
"Just to be needed is more sweet," says she,
"Than any freedom in this world could be."

MARY EVERSLEY

COUNT TEN

(Count ten before speaking in anger.)

What shall we count to cool our angry pride?
Ten chilly digits standing in a line?
Oh, wiser far to count ten circling stars
That lean upon blue space: they will decline
To lend themselves to bitterness or pain.
Or we might count ten muted leaves that fall
Bearing a freight of somber autumn rain—
Ten leaves that fall, one here, one distantly,
In leisurely submission to the ground.
Or ten flecked pebbles lying in a pool
So hushed by dawn that the air holds no sound

Of water-motion. Or count ten mortal men
Who have come forth by the red gate of birth
To meet the wind . . . to learn the tang of laughter . . .
To wonder . . . and return into the earth.
For having counted, slowly we can lift
Our eyes to look on him who has offended,
Saying, "How large and strange this life we live . . .
Was I enraged with you? . . . Well, that is ended . . ."

BONARO OVERSTREET

A PRAYER FOR FAITH

God, give me back the simple faith that I so long have clung
 to,
 My simple faith in peace and hope, in loveliness and
  light—
Because without this faith of mine, the rhythms I have sung
 to
 Become as empty as the sky upon a starless night.

God, let me feel that right is right, that reason dwells with
 reason,
 And let me feel that something grows whenever there is
  rain—
And let me sense the splendid truth that season follows
 season,
 And let me dare to dream that there is tenderness in pain.

355

God, give me back my simple faith because my soul is
    straying
  Away from all the little creeds that I so long have known;
Oh, answer me while still I have at least the strength for
    praying,
  For if the prayer dies from my heart I will be quite alone.

MARGARET E. SANGSTER

THE WORLD WE MAKE

We make the world in which we live
By what we gather and what we give,
By our daily deeds and the things we say,
By what we keep or we cast away.

We make our world by the beauty we see
In a skylark's song or a lilac tree,
In a butterfly's wing, in the pale moon's rise,
And the wonder that lingers in midnight skies.

We make our world by the life we lead,
By the friends we have, by the books we read,
By the pity we show in the hour of care,
By the loads we lift and the love we share.

We make our world by the goals we pursue,
By the heights we seek and the higher view,
By hopes and dreams that reach the sun
And a will to fight till the heights are won.

What is the place in which we dwell,
A hut or a palace, a heaven or hell
We gather and scatter, we take and we give,
We make our world—and there we live.

ALFRED GRANT WALTON

MEDIATION No. 2979

MEDIATORS

Miss Fannie Hurst—*Novelist*
Mr. Martin W. Littleton—*Attorney*
Dr. Phillips P. Elliott—*President, Brooklyn Federation of Churches*

A man deeply hurt, soured by life, had been told during the course of a proceeding to which he was a party that for his own sake he must try to face the future with some measure of hopefulness and courage. Admittedly he had experienced many hardships and anxieties, but perhaps he could acknowledge there was something yet remaining for which he could be thankful. The next day he wrote me a long letter, part of which I quote: "You and your board speak of courage. Perhaps you wouldn't if you were in my place. I had a wife—an invalid. For years I tried to nurse her puny, suffering body back to health. Three weeks ago she was operated on and died. Others are dependent upon me for

357

their existence. Not that it matters now, but with nothing but darkness and debts to look forward to—I find myself laid off my job. People say there is a God. What have I to thank him for?"

Saddened by this unhappy, embittered man, I searched for an answer to his question and asked myself, what, indeed, is there to thank God for in the face of such calamity and disillusionment? On the next program I read this poem:

THANK GOD!

Thank God for life!
E'en though it bring much bitterness and strife,
    And all our fairest hopes be wrecked and lost,
E'en though there be more ill than good in life,
    We cling to life and reckon not the cost.
        Thank God for life!

Thank God for love!
For though sometimes grief follows in its wake,
    Still we forget love's sorrow in love's joy,
And cherish tears with smiles for love's dear sake;
    Only in heaven is bliss without alloy.
        Thank God for love!

Thank God for pain!
No tear hath ever yet been shed in vain,
    And in the end each sorrowing heart shall find
No curse, but blessings in the hand of pain;
    Even when he smiteth, then is God most kind.
        Thank God for pain!

Thank God for death!
Who touches anguished lips and stills their breath
    And giveth peace unto each troubled breast;
Grief flies before thy touch, O blessed death;
    God's sweetest gift; thy name in heaven is Rest.
        Thank God for death!

AUTHOR UNKNOWN

BE PATIENT

They are such dear familiar feet that go
Along the path with ours—feet fast or slow
But trying to keep pace; if they mistake
Or tread upon some flower that we would take
Upon our breast, or bruise some reed,
Or crush poor hope until it bleed,
We must be mute;
Not turning quickly to impute
Grave fault: for they and we
Have such a little way to go, can be
Together such a little while upon the way—
We must be patient while we may.

So many little faults we find.
We see them, for not blind

Is love. We see them, but if you and I
Perhaps remember them, some by and by,
They will not be
Faults then, grave faults, to you and me,
But just odd ways, mistakes, or even less—
Remembrances to bless.
Days change so many things, yes, hours;
We see so differently in sun and showers!
Mistaken words tonight
May be so cherished by tomorrow's light—
We shall be patient, for we know
There's such a little way to go.

GEORGE KLINGLE

A DOG'S VIGIL

There is a friendship that exists between
   So-called dumb animals; we often find
Them sorrowing with a grief that is as keen
   And deeply felt as those of humankind.

For many times this has been plainly shown
   To me, and yet more clearly when I read
The story of a dog who kept alone,
   A vigil when his mongrel pal lay dead.

Just how his pal met death I never knew—
  I know he kept a lonely watch all day,
Through bitter cold, and not until he grew
  Exhausted, would he let friends take away

The comrade he had known in happy hours;
  No human could have shown more faithfulness;
He could not tell his grief with words or flowers,
  But only with a puzzled, mute distress.

And when kind ones returned who bore away
  His lifeless friend, no watcher was in sight. . . .
But travelers through a neighboring field, they say,
  Had seen a lonely dog pass by that night.

                                MARGARET E. BRUNER

THE DREAMS AHEAD

What would we do in this world of ours
  Were it not for the dreams ahead?
For thorns are mixed with the blooming flowers
  No matter which path we tread.

And each of us has his golden goal,
  Stretching far into the years;
And ever he climbs with a hopeful soul,
  With alternate smiles and tears.

That dream ahead is what holds him up
  Through the storms of a ceaseless fight;
When his lips are pressed to the wormwood's cup
  And clouds shut out the light.

To some it's a dream of high estate;
  To some it's a dream of wealth;
To some it's a dream of a truce with Fate
  In a constant search for health.

To some it's a dream of home and wife;
  To some it's a crown above;
The dreams ahead are what make each life—
  The dreams—and faith—and love!

                              EDWIN CARLILE LITSEY

SONS OF PROMISE

  In every meanest face I see
  A perfected humanity;
  All men, though brothers of the clod,
  Bear promise of the sons of God.

  No human ore that does not hold
  A precious element of gold;
  No heart so blackened and debased
  But has for Him some treasure chaste.

                      THOMAS CURTIS CLARK

FRIENDS

If all the sorrows of this weary earth—
  The pains and heartaches of humanity—
  If all were gathered up and given me,
I still would have my share of wealth and worth
  Who have you, Friend of Old, to be my cheer
  Through life's uncertain fortunes, year by year.

Thank God for friends, who dearer grow as years increase;
  Who, as possessions fail our hopes and hands,
  Become the boon supreme, than gold and lands
More precious. Let all else, if must be, cease;
  But, Lord of Life, I pray on me bestow
  The gift of friends, to share the way I go.

THOMAS CURTIS CLARK

MEDIATION No. 7398

MEDIATORS

Hon. Albert Goldman—*Postmaster of New York*
Dr. Wilfred J. Funk—*President of Wilfred Funk, Inc., Book Publishers*
David Seabury—*Psychologist*

This is the very human story of a man of considerable worth who had the misfortune to be enslaved by drink—a chronic alcoholic. We are all familiar with stories of broken little families, ruined by factors quite unexpected. This young husband and father had become bitterly disillusioned because of the faithlessness of the one person in the world he trusted—his wife. To forget his utter misery he turned to drink, losing all interest in his home, his business, deliberately throwing away a brilliant and honorable career. Resigned to his fate, he permitted himself to be dragged into the depths of degradation. Every effort was made to keep liquor from him, but somehow he managed to accomplish this purpose of "drowning his sorrow."

While of course no board could propose to cure such a situation, the fact is that cures for chronic alcoholism have often been effected by various means, including medicine, psychiatry, religion, or by a combination of all three, when the victim himself has been willing to recognize the possibility of cure and has lent his complete co-operation to the treatment planned for him. Up to this time the man had shown no interest in so doing, having lost all faith in the essential fairness and goodness of life. Finally he was approached on the basis of his love for his child and its future welfare. With the family broken up, the child, a manly little chap of four, was about to be placed in a home.

So successful was the aftermath of this case (the man having agreed to place himself in competent hands and thus co-operate toward the overcoming of his dread craving for drink) that he finally achieved a splendid victory over himself, forgave his deeply repentant spouse and, with his health, confidence and self-respect restored, is again with his family on the road to happiness. When disillusionment and hardship cause love to grow cold so many relationships conceivably could overcome a period of great danger, perhaps go on to great success, if people could be taken out of themselves to extend the hand of forgiveness in the common cause of a child. The poem read on the occasion this case was originally heard was titled *Two Prayers*.

TWO PRAYERS

Last night my little boy confessed to me
Some childish wrong;
And kneeling at my knee,
He prayed with tears—
"Dear God, make me a man
Like Daddy—wise and strong;
I know you can."

Then while he slept
I knelt beside his bed,
Confessed my sins,
And prayed with low-bowed head.
"O God, make me a child
Like my child here—
Pure, guileless,
Trusting Thee with faith sincere."

ANDREW GILLIES

WE KISS'D AGAIN WITH TEARS

As through the land at eve we went,
　　And pluck'd the ripen'd ears,
We fell out, my wife and I,
O we fell out I know not why,
　　And kiss'd again with tears.
And blessings on the falling out
　　That all the more endears,
When we fall out with those we love,
　　And kiss again with tears!
For when we came where lies the child
　　We lost in other years,
There above the little grave,
O there above the little grave,
　　We kiss'd again with tears.

FROM "THE PRINCESS"
BY ALFRED LORD TENNYSON

LET HIM RETURN

Who, in the brief, incredible northern spring,
Has watched plum petals fall and pear bloom go,
And has observed the sun's slow subtle swing
Toward high summer, and seen blackberry snow
Drifting in swamps where wild blue flags are tall,
Let him return in the acrid, windy fall.

Let him return when color runs and spills
Across the land he loved; let him return
When smoke lies purple on the shadowy hills
Of a lifted country where the maples burn
Scarlet in upland woods and dark birds cry
Poised on a curve of gusty autumn sky.

LEONA AMES HILL

DISCOVERY

I wished to shirk my task one day:
I much preferred some pleasant play.
But when the work I'd once begun,
'Twas full of interest, joy and fun.

The dust removed from off my books
Brought happy thoughts and cheerful looks.
Weeds, in the garden, put to rout,
Made beauty blossom round about.

Why use my time and strength and skill
In hard-wrought play, to serve me ill?
Why from sure pleasure should I shirk,
Since there is play in pleasant work?

BENJAMIN KEECH

TRUE TO THE BEST

Long years of pleasant friendship may be broken
  By one hour's work with thoughtless word or deed.
Yet why forget the thousand good words spoken,
  The kindly help which met a passing need?

We do not spurn the sunlight when 'tis hidden;
  We look for good when fiercest storms descend.
Then why lose faith, when undeserved, unbidden,
  We meet disloyal usage from a friend?

BENJAMIN KEECH

LITTLE ROADS TO HAPPINESS

The little roads to happiness, they are not hard to find;
They do not lead to great success—but to a quiet mind.
They do not lead to mighty power, nor to substantial wealth.
They bring one to a book, a flower, a song of cheer and
    health.
The little roads to happiness are free to everyone;
They lead one to the wind's caress, to kiss of friendly sun.
These little roads are shining white, for all the world to see;
Their sign-boards, pointing left and right, are love and
    sympathy.
The little roads of happiness have this most charming way;
No matter how they may digress throughout the busy day;
No matter where they twist and wind through fields of rich
    delight,
They're always of the self same mind to lead us home at
    night.

WILHELMINA STITCH

*For he that will love life, and see good days, let him re-
frain his tongue from evil, and his lips that they speak no
guile.*

1 PETER 3:10

THE TONGUE

"The boneless tongue, so small and weak,
Can crush and kill," declares the Greek.
"The tongue destroys a greater hoard,"
The Turk asserts, "than does the sword."

A Persian proverb wisely saith,
"A lengthy tongue—an early death";
Or sometimes takes this form instead,
"Don't let your tongue cut off your head."

"The tongue can speak a word whose speed,"
The Chinese say, "outstrips the steed";
While Arab sages this impart,
"The tongue's great storehouse is the heart."

From Hebrew wit this maxim sprung,
"Though feet should slip, ne'er let the tongue."
The sacred writer crowns the whole,
"Who keeps his tongue doth keep his soul!"

AUTHOR UNKNOWN

AT SUNRISE

They pushed him straight against the wall;
   The firing squad dropped in a row;
And why he stood on tiptoes,
   Those men shall never know.

He wore a smile across his face
   As he stood primly there,
The guns straight aiming at his heart,
   The sun upon his hair;

For he remembered, in a flash,
   Those days beyond recall,
When his proud mother took his height
   Against the bedroom wall.

ROSA ZAGNONI MARINONI

QUESTION NOT

Question not, but live and labor,
   Till your goal be won,
Helping every feeble neighbor,
   Seeking help from none;

Life is mostly froth and bubble,
　Two things stand like stone—
Kindness in another's trouble,
　Courage in our own.

ADAM LINDSAY GORDON

UNDERSTANDING

Not more of light I ask, O God,
　But eyes to see what is:
Not sweeter songs, but ears to hear
　The present melodies:
Not more of strength, but how to use
　The power that I possess:
Not more of love, but skill to turn
　A frown to a caress:
Not more of joy, but how to feel
　Its kindly presence near
To give to others all I have
　Of courage and of cheer.

No other gifts, dear God, I ask,
　But only sense to see
How best these precious gifts to use
　Thou hast bestowed on me.

AUTHOR UNKNOWN

I AM STILL RICH

I am still rich.
The morning comes with old-time cheer;
The sun breaks through the blurring mist;
And all the sorrows of the night
By newborn rays of hope are kissed.
Up and rejoice! a spirit cries,
What is your loss, with morning skies!

I am still rich.
My friends are faithful, as of old;
They trust me past my poor desert.
They ask no gift of golden gain,
But only love. With their strength girt,
Can I not face the road ahead—
Though some old treasured joys are dead!

I am still rich.
I have my work, which constant calls;
I could not loiter, if I would;
Each moment has some task to speed,
Some work to do. How kind, how good
Is life that God now grants to me—
A segment of Eternity!

THOMAS CURTIS CLARK

I KNOW SOMETHING GOOD ABOUT YOU

Wouldn't this old world be better
  If the folks we meet would say—
"I know something good about you!"
  And treat us just that way?

Wouldn't it be fine and dandy
  If each handclasp, fond and true,
Carried with it this assurance—
  "I know something good about you!"

Wouldn't life be lots more happy
  If the good that's in us all
Were the only thing about us
  That folks bothered to recall?

Wouldn't life be lots more happy
  If we praised the good we see?
For there's such a lot of goodness
  In the worst of you and me!

Wouldn't it be nice to practice
  That fine way of thinking, too?
You know something good about me;
  I know something good about you.

AUTHOR UNKNOWN

WAS, IS, AND YET-TO-BE

Was, Is, and Yet-to-be
Were chatting, over a cup of tea.

In tarnished finery smelling of must,
Was talked of people long turned to dust;

Of titles and honors and high estate,
All forgotten or out of date;

Of wonderful feasts in the long ago,
Of pride that perished with nothing to show.

"I loathe the present," said Was, with a groan,
"I live in pleasures that I have known."

The Yet-to-be, in a gown of gauze,
Looked over the head of musty Was,

And gazed far off into misty space
With a wrapt expression upon her face.

"Such wonderful pleasures are coming to me,
Such glory, such honor," said Yet-to-be.

"No one dreamed in the vast has-been
Of such successes as I shall win.

The past, the present, why what are they?
I live for the glory of a future day."

Then practical Is, in a fresh print dress,
Spoke up with a laugh, "I must confess

I find today so pleasant," she said;
"I never look back, and seldom ahead.

Whatever has been, is a finished sum;
Whatever will be, why let it come.

Today is mine. And so you see
I have the past and the yet to be;

For today is the future of yesterday,
And the past of tomorrow. I live while I may,

And I think the secret of pleasure is this,
And this alone," said practical Is.

ELLA WHEELER WILCOX

My crown is in my heart, not on my head;
Not deck'd with diamonds and Indian stones,
Nor to be seen: my crown is call'd content.
FROM *King Henry VI* BY WILLIAM SHAKESPEARE

BLESSED ARE THEY

Blessed are they who are pleasant to live with—
Blessed are they who sing in the morning;
Whose faces have smiles for their early adorning;
Who come down to breakfast companioned by cheer;
Who don't dwell on troubles or entertain fear;
Whose eyes smile forth bravely; whose lips curve to say:
"Life, I salute you! Good morrow, new day!"
Blessed are they who are pleasant to live with—
Blessed are they who treat one another,
Though merely a sister, a father or brother,
With the very same courtesy they would extend
To a casual acquaintance or dearly loved friend;
Who choose for the telling encouraging things;
Who choke back the bitter, the sharp word that stings;
Who bestow love on others throughout the long day—
Pleasant to live with and blessed are they.

WILHELMINA STITCH

We live in deeds, not years; in thoughts, not breaths;
 In feelings, not in figures on a dial.
We should count time by heart-throbs. He most lives
 Who thinks most—feels the noblest—acts the best.

FROM "A COUNTRY TOWN" BY PHILIP JAMES BAILEY

GIVING

God gives us joy that we may give;
  He gives us joy that we may share;
Sometimes He gives us loads to lift
  That we may learn to bear.
For life is gladder when we give,
  And love is sweeter when we share,
And heavy loads rest lightly too
  When we have learned to bear.

AUTHOR UNKNOWN

Despise not any man that lives,
Alien or neighbor, near or far;
Go out beneath the scornful stars,
And see how very small you are.
The world is large, and space is high
That sweeps around our little ken;
But there's no space or time to spare
In which to hate our fellow men.
And this, my friend, is not the work for you;
Then leave all this for smaller men to do.

FROM "WORK FOR SMALL MEN"

BY SAM WALTER FOSS

THE POWER OF PRAYER

Lord, what a change within us one short hour
  Spent in Thy presence will avail to make!
  What heavy burdens from our bosoms take;
What parched grounds refresh, as with a shower!
We kneel, and all around us seems to lower;
  We rise, and all, the distant and the near,
  Stands forth in sunny outline, brave and clear!
We kneel, how weak! We rise, how full of power!

Why, therefore, should we do ourselves this wrong
Or others, that we are not always strong;
That we are ever overborne with care;
  That we should ever weak or heartless be,
Anxious or troubled, when with us is prayer,
  And joy and strength and courage are with Thee?
                    RICHARD CHEVENIX TRENCH

MOTHER

As long ago we carried to your knees
The tales and treasures of eventful days,
Knowing no deed too humble for your praise,
Nor any gift too trivial to please,

So still we bring with older smiles and tears,
What gifts we may to claim the old, dear right;
Your faith beyond the silence and the night;
Your love still close and watching through the years.

AUTHOR UNKNOWN

The quality of FRIENDSHIP—*is the melody and fragrance of life—And the oil in the lamp of friendship is faith! Without faith, there can be no friendship or anything else. By that faith, the flame of life is kept burning.*

MY FRIENDS ARE LITTLE LAMPS TO ME

My friends are little lamps to me,
   Their radiance warms and cheers my ways.
And all my pathway dark and lone
   Is brightened by their rays.

I try to keep them bright by faith,
   And never let them dim with doubt,
For every time I lose a friend
   A little lamp goes out.

ELIZABETH WHITTEMORE

MODERATION

"He that holds fast the golden mean,
And lives contentedly between
  The little and the great,
Feels not the wants that pinch the poor,
Nor plagues that haunt the rich man's door
  Embittering all his state."
  WILLIAM COWPER, TRANSLATION OF HORACE,
                          ODES, BOOK II

TO MY FRIEND

I have never been rich before,
  But you have poured
Into my heart's high door
  A golden hoard.

My wealth is the vision shared,
  The sympathy,
The feast of the soul prepared
  By you for me.

Together we wander through
  The wooded ways.
Old beauties are green and new
  Seen through your gaze.

I look for no greater prize
  Than your soft voice.
The steadiness of your eyes
  Is my heart's choice.

I have never been rich before,
  But I divine
Your step on my sunlit floor
  And wealth is mine!

ANNE CAMPBELL

VISIT THE SICK

There is no person lonelier . . . Than he who lies in bed . . . And must depend on others . . . To be comfortable and fed . . . Who never has a visitor . . . To talk to him and smile . . . And make the life he has to live . . . A little more worth while . . . He does not ask for magazines . . . For candy, fruit and such . . . But just a friendly visit and . . . The words that mean so much . . . He wants to see the sun come out . . . In place of all the rain . . . And know that someone cares about . . . His trouble and his pain . . . And surely somewhere out of all . . . The moments made for play . . . There must be time to call on him . . . And say hello today.

JAMES J. METCALFE

AN ANGRY WORD

An angry word is like a boomerang;
  Its force returns upon the one who sent it,
And yet unlike it, for it has a fang
  Whose poison doubles after one has spent it.

MARGARET E. BRUNER

GUIDE-POSTS ON THE FOOTPATH TO PEACE

To be glad of life because it gives you the chance to love and to work and to play and to look up at the stars; to be satisfied with your possessions, but not contented with yourself until you have made the best of them; to despise nothing in the world except falsehood and meanness, and to fear nothing except cowardice; to be governed by your admirations rather than by your disgusts; to covet nothing that is your neighbor's except his kindness of heart and gentleness of manner; to think seldom of your enemies, often of your friends and every day of God, and to spend as much time as you can with body and with spirit in God's out-of-doors—these are the little guide-posts on the footpath to peace.

HENRY VAN DYKE

ACKNOWLEDGMENTS

The publisher has made every effort to trace the owner-ship of all copyrighted poems. It is his belief that the necessary permissions from authors or their authorized agents have been obtained in all cases. In the event of any question arising as to the use of any poem, the publisher, while expressing regret for any error he has unconsciously made, will be pleased to make the necessary correction in future editions of this book.

Thanks are due to the following authors, publishers, publications and agents for permission to use the poems indicated:

American Poetry Magazine of Wisconsin—for "The Greater Gift", by Margaret E. Bruner.

American Tract Society—for an excerpt from "Bees in Amber", by John Oxenham.

D. Appleton-Century Co.—for a brief excerpt from William Cullen Bryant's "Thanatopsis".

Estate of John Kendrick Bangs—for "Philosophy"; "On File", from Songs of Cheer, by John Kendrick Bangs.

Braley, Berton—for "That's Success" and "Start Where You Stand".

Brethren Publishing House—for "The Touch of the Master's Hand", by Myra Brooks Welch, copyright, 1943, by Brethren Publishing House.

Bruner, Margaret E.—for "One Lately Bereft", "Midwinter", "Time's Hand Is Kind", "Beyond the Grave", "Remembrance", and "Rebirth", from Indianapolis Sunday Star; "Wedding Anniversary", from Indiana Poetry Magazine; "Prayer for

Acknowledgments

Strength" and "The Greater Gift", from *American Poetry Magazine;* "The Gift", "The Monk and the Peasant", "Selfishness", "The Sinner", "The Beggar", "Good-by", and "There Is a Loneliness", from THE HILL ROAD; "Casual Meeting" and "An Angry Word", from MIDSTREAM; "If Lincoln Should Return", "Atonement", "On City Streets", "The Dreaded Task", "God's Ways Are Strange", and "A Dog's Vigil", from IN THOUGHTFUL MOOD; "The Lonely Dog", from MYSTERIES OF EARTH; "Plea for Tolerance", from BE SLOW TO FALTER; "For One Who Is Serene", from THE CONSTANT HEART.

Campbell, Anne—for "To My Friend"; "There Is Always a Place for You"; "Shabby Old Dad", copyright, 1947, by Anne Campbell; "Before and After Marriage", copyright, 1947, by Anne Campbell.

Chamberlin, Katherine—for "Resolve", by Charlotte P. S. Gilman.

Christian Science Monitor and Leona Ames Hill—for "Let Him Return", by Leona Ames Hill.

Clark, Thomas Curtis—for "I Am Still Rich" and "Take Time to Live", from HOME ROADS AND FAR HORIZONS; "The Touch of Human Hands" and "God's Dreams", from 1000 QUOTABLE POEMS; "Friends", from ABRAHAM LINCOLN: FIFTY POEMS.

Conklin, Margaret—for "The Philosopher", by Sara Teasdale.

Cornhill Publishing Co.—for "Who Builds a Church", by Morris Abel Beer.

Davies, Mary Carolyn—for "To Give One's Life", "A Vow for New Year's", "A Prayer for Every Day", "Let Me Be a Giver".

de Leeuw, Adele—for "Auction Sale—Household Furnishings".

The Devin-Adair Company—for "The Old Woman", by Joseph Campbell, from 1000 YEARS OF IRISH POETRY, edited by Kathleen Hoagland, copyright, 1947, by The Devin-Adair Company.

Dodd, Mead & Company, Inc.—for "Aloha Oe", from VAGABOND'S HOUSE, copyright, 1928, by Don Blanding; renewal copyright, © 1956, by Don Blanding.

E. P. Dutton & Co., Inc.—for "Dusk", by Helen Welshimer, from SINGING DRUMS.

For "Blessed Are They" and "Little Roads to Happiness", by

Wilhelmina Stitch, from Sɪʟᴋᴇɴ Tʜʀᴇᴀᴅs, copyright, 1930, by E. P. Dutton & Co., Inc.

For "Husband and Wife" and "Welcome Over the Door of an Old Inn", by Arthur Guiterman, from Dᴇᴀᴛʜ ᴀɴᴅ Gᴇɴᴇʀᴀʟ Pᴜᴛɴᴀᴍ, copyright, 1935, by E. P. Dutton & Co., Inc.

Ehrmann, Max—for "Mother", "Away", and "A Prayer".

Fuller, Ethel Romig—for "What the King Has"; for "Today", from Kɪᴛᴄʜᴇɴ Sᴏɴɴᴇᴛs, copyright, 1956, by Ethel Romig Fuller.

Funk, Wilfred—for "Hospital".

Gillilan, Strickland—for "Be Hopeful", "Need of Loving", "Watch Yourself Go By" (Rhodeheaver Publishing Co.).

Guiterman, Mrs. Arthur—for "The Whole Duty of a Poem", by Arthur Guiterman, copyright, by Arthur Guiterman.

Harcourt, Brace & Co.—for "Prayer for This House", by Louis Untermeyer, from Tʜɪs Sɪɴɢɪɴɢ Wᴏʀʟᴅ.

Harper & Brothers—for the following poems by Grace Noll Crowell: "Courage to Live", from Tʜɪs Gᴏʟᴅᴇɴ Sᴜᴍᴍɪᴛ; "A Day's Walk", "Eternal Values", "I Have Found Such Joy", and "Definition", from Lɪɢʜᴛ ᴏғ ᴛʜᴇ Yᴇᴀʀs, copyright, 1936, by Harper & Brothers; "The Common Tasks", from Sᴏɴɢs ᴏғ Hᴏᴘᴇ, copyright, 1938, by Harper & Brothers.

For "Recipe for Living", by Alfred Grant Walton, from Hɪɢʜᴡᴀʏs Tᴏ Hᴀᴘᴘɪɴᴇss, copyright, 1938, by Harper & Brothers.

Harper's Magazine—for "My Friends Are Little Lamps to Me", by Elizabeth Whittemore, copyright, 1923, 1951, by Harper & Brothers.

Hicky, Daniel Whitehead—for "No Friend Like Music" and "When a Man Turns Homeward".

Hines, Nellie Womack—for "Home", from Hᴏᴍᴇ-Kᴇᴇᴘɪɴɢ Hᴇᴀʀᴛs, A Book of Verse by Nellie Womack Hines.

Holmes, John—for "Good Night! Good Night!" (Courtesy of the New York *Times*).

Henry Holt & Co., Inc.—for "At a Window", by Carl Sandburg, from Cʜɪᴄᴀɢᴏ Pᴏᴇᴍs.

Acknowledgments

Houghton Mifflin Company—for "Next Year" and "Too Late", by Nora Perry, from NEW SONGS AND BALLADS.

For "Hymn", by Harriet Beecher Stowe.

For "Our Opportunity Today", by Celia Thaxter.

For "My Wage", by Jessie B. Rittenhouse, from DOOR OF DREAMS, copyright, 1918, by Jessie B. Rittenhouse; copyright, 1946, by Jessie B. Rittenhouse Scollard.

For "The Story of Life" and "The Blind Men and the Elephant", by John G. Saxe.

Bruce Humphries, Inc.—for "The Hate and the Love of the World", "I Ponder O'er Love" and "If You Made Gentler the Churlish World", by Max Ehrmann, from THE POEMS OF MAX EHRMANN, copyright, 1948, by Bertha K. Ehrmann.

The Kaleidograph Press, Dallas, Texas—for "Rendezvous", by Mary Scott Fitzgerald.

For "Plea for Tolerance", by Margaret E. Bruner, from BE SLOW TO FALTER; "For One Who Is Serene", by Margaret E. Bruner, from THE CONSTANT HEART.

Keith, Joseph Joel—for "Definitions".

P. J. Kenedy & Sons—for "A Builder's Lesson", by John Boyle O'Reilly, from SELECTED POEMS, copyright, 1913, by John Boyle O'Reilly.

Kennerley, Mitchell—for "The Closed Door", by Theodosia Garrison.

King Features Syndicate, Inc.—for the following poems by Elsie Robinson: "Help Me Today", "Beauty as a Shield", and "Pain", © King Features Syndicate, Inc.

Kiser, Samuel E.—for "Unsubdued" and "My Creed".

Alfred A. Knopf, Inc.—for excerpts from "Crime and Punishment", "On Work", and "On Children", from THE PROPHET, by Kahlil Gibran, copyright, 1923, by Kahlil Gibran; renewal copyright, 1951, by Administrators C.T.A. of Kahlil Gibran Estate and Mary G. Gibran.

Little, Brown & Co.—for "If I Can Stop One Heart from Breaking", by Emily Dickinson, from THE POEMS OF EMILY DICKINSON, edited by Martha Dickinson Bianchi and Alfred Leete Hampson.

388

Acknowledgments

For "Shall I Complain?", by Louise Chandler Moulton, from AT THE WIND'S WILL.

For "Fate", by Susan Marr Spalding, from THE WINGS OF ICARUS.

Lothrop, Lee Shepard Co.—for "Work for Small Men", by Sam Walter Foss, from WHIFFS FROM WILD MEADOWS.

F. Alexander Magoun—for "Goodnight (for Husbands and Wives)", copyright, 1936, by F. Alexander Magoun.

Marinoni, Rosa Zagnoni—for "At Sunrise" (Kaleidograph Press); "Who Are My People", "For the New Home".

Markham, Virgil—for "Outwitted" and "The Right Kind of People", by Edwin Markham.

Mase, Sidney Warren—for "It's Simply Great" (Forbes Magazine).

Masters, Mrs. Edgar Lee—for "Silence", by Edgar Lee Masters, from SONGS AND SATIRES, copyright, 1918, The Macmillan Company.

David McKay Co., Inc.—for "Destiny", by Sir Edwin Arnold.

For the following poems by Ella Wheeler Wilcox: "Faith", "Will", "Life", "Optimism", "Mistakes", "Worth While", "Friendship", "One of Us Two", "A Morning Prayer", "Two Kinds of People", "You Never Can Tell", "Whatever Is—Is Best", "Was, Is, and Yet-to-be", "Those We Love the Best", "Accept My Heart's Thanks".

Metcalfe, James J.—for "Visit the Sick", from POEM PORTRAITS, copyright, 1948, by James J. Metcalfe.

Miller, Juanita—for "For Those Who Fail", by Joaquin Miller.

John Murray (Publishers) Ltd. of London—for "Why Do I Live", by Thomas Guthrie.

Newell, Catherine Parmenter—for "Dream House", which originally appeared in the magazine *Columbia*.

Noble & Noble Publishers, Inc.—for "Life's Mirror", by Madeline Bridges, from THE BRIGHT SIDE.

W. W. Norton & Company, Inc.—for "Count Ten", by Bonaro Overstreet, from HANDS LAID UPON THE WIND, copyright, 1955, by W. W. Norton & Company, Inc.

Acknowledgments

L. C. Page & Co.—for "The Bridge Builder", by Will Allen Dromgoole, from RARE CHUMS.

Peabody, Josephine Fish—for "A Last Will", by Williston Fish.

The Reilly & Lee Co.—"The Kindly Neighbor", by Edgar A. Guest, from ALL THAT MATTERS; "What's in It for Me?", by Edgar A. Guest, from COLLECTED VERSE, copyright, 1934, by The Reilly & Lee Co.; "Equipment", by Edgar A. Guest, from HARBOR LIGHTS OF HOME, copyright, 1928, by The Reilly & Lee Co.

Fleming H. Revell Co.—for "The House of Pride", by William J. Dawson.

For "The Pendulum", by Dwight Lyman Moody.

Reynolds, Lucile Hargrove—for "To the New Owner" (Courtesy of the *Saturday Evening Post*).

Robinson, Elsie—for "Beauty as a Shield" and "Pain", copyright, © King Features Syndicate, Inc.

Rowswell, Mrs. Albert K.—for "Should You Go First", by Albert K. Rowswell, from ROSEY REFLECTIONS, copyrighted.

Sangster, Margaret E.—for "Forgiven", "Our Own", "Face to Face with Trouble", "Sin of Omission", "A Prayer for Faith", "The Blind Man", and "Patience with the Living".

Charles Scribner's Sons—for "Four Things", by Henry Van Dyke.

Searle, Ora—for "Nightfall", by Charles Hanson Towne, copyrighted.

Stidger, William L.—for "Day", from I SAW GOD WASH THE WORLD (Rhodeheaver-Hall-Mack Co., Philadelphia, Pa.) and "Lest Thou Forget".

Storey, Violet Alleyn—for "Prayer for Broken Little Families", from TEA IN AN OLD HOUSE.

Wagner, Charles L. H.—for "Let's Forget", from PAINTED ROCKS.

Walton, Alfred Grant—for "First Impressions", "The World We Make", "Recipe for Living", from HIGHWAYS TO HAPPINESS, copyright, 1938, by Harper & Brothers; "The Sincere Man", from SONGS FOR THE SEASON, copyright, 1948, by Alfred Grant Walton.

Wells, Carolyn—for "Alone".

Acknowledgments

Williams, B. Y.—for "The Friend that Just Stands By", from HOUSE OF HAPPINESS.

Wm. H. Wise & Co., Inc.—for "Because You Care", by Frank Crane, from EVERYDAY WISDOM, copyrighted.

INDEX OF AUTHORS

INDEX OF TITLES

INDEX OF FIRST LINES

Index of First Lines

Index of First Lines

Index of First Lines